# THE CHURCH AT WORSHIP: CASE STUDIES FROM CHRISTIAN HISTORY

Series Editors: LESTER RUTH, CARRIE STEENWYK, JOHN D. WITVLIET

## Published

*Walking Where Jesus Walked: Worship in Fourth-Century Jerusalen*
Lester Ruth, Carrie Steenwyk, John D. Witvliet

*Tasting Heaven on Earth: Worship in Sixth-Century Constantinople*
Walter D. Ray

*Longing for Jesus: Worship at a Black Holiness Church
in Mississippi, 1895–1913*
Lester Ruth

*Lifting Hearts to the Lord: Worship with John Calvin
in Sixteenth-Century Geneva*
Karin Maag

*Worshiping with the Anaheim Vineyard: The Emergence
of Contemporary Worship*
Andy Park, Lester Ruth, and Cindy Rethmeier

## Forthcoming

*Joining Hearts and Voices: Worship with Isaac Watts
in Eighteenth-Century London*
Christopher J. Ellis

*Leaning On the Word: Worship with Argentine Baptists
in the Mid-Twentieth Century*
Lester Ruth and Eric Mathis

# Worshiping with the

# Anaheim Vineyard

The Emergence of Contemporary Worship

ANDY PARK, LESTER RUTH, AND CINDY RETHMEIER

William B. Eerdmans Publishing Company
Grand Rapids, Michigan

Wm. B. Eerdmans Publishing Co.
2140 Oak Industrial Drive N.E., Grand Rapids, Michigan 49505
www.eerdmans.com

22  21  20  19  18  17          1  2  3  4  5  6  7

ISBN 978-0-8028-7397-2

**Library of Congress Cataloging-in-Publication Data**

A catalog record for this book is available from the Library of Congress

# Contents

Series Introduction   viii

Suggestions for Complementary Reading   xi

Acknowledgments   xiii


PART ONE: LOCATING THE WORSHIPING COMMUNITY

The Context of the Worshiping Community: Anaheim Vineyard Fellowship, 1977–1983   3

Timeline   12

Liturgical Landscape   16

Geographical Landscape   19

Cautions for Studying Anaheim Vineyard's Worship History   20

Significant Themes and Practices to Observe   22


PART TWO: EXPLORING THE WORSHIPING COMMUNITY

Describing the Community's Worship: Questions and Answers with Andy Park   29

Documenting the Community's Worship   47

  People and Artifacts   47

    The Anaheim Vineyard Congregation in the Early 1980s   47

    The Anaheim Vineyard Congregation Worshiping   48

    The Worship Team   49

    John Wimber Addresses the Congregation   50

    Prayer Ministry among Vineyard Worshipers   51

    The Worship Team Leading Worship   52

    Weekly Schedule for Worship and Church Life   53

    Songs of the Vineyard Cover and Advertisement   54

    Schedule for the 1981 Trip to South Africa   55

    1982 Trip to England   56

    Notice for 1984 Worship Conference   57

Worship Setting and Space   58

  *Freedom of Expression*   58

  *A Sea of Worshipers*   59

  *The Musicians' Platform from the Side*   60

  *Later Arrangement of Space*   61

Descriptions of Worship   62

  *Worship in a Home: Origins of the Anaheim Vineyard Congregation*   62

  *Testimonies from Early Participants*   67

  *Early Participants' Recollections about the Music*   70

  *Worshipers Describe the Dramatic Ministry of the Holy Spirit during Worship*   75

  *Reports on Worship from Early Church Planters*   80

Order of Service and Texts   82

  *A Representative Song*   82

  *Some Songs Written by John Wimber*   83

  *Anaheim Vineyard's Song Repertoire*   85

  *Songs from the 1982 Album*   86

Sermons   87

  *John Wimber's Sermon on "Loving God"*   87

  *Excerpts from "Why Do We Worship?"*   102

  *Excerpts from "Don't Lose Your First Love"*   104

  *Excerpts from "Essence of Worship"*   106

Theology of Worship Documents   109

  *Outline of Vineyard Teaching*   109

  *Wimber's Understanding of Worship as God-Given Destiny*   113

  *Wimber Teaches Worship as Abandonment to God*   113

  *Teaching on the Corporate Nature of Worship*   115

  *The Church's Pragmatism Shapes Planning*   115

  *The Phases of Worship*   117

  *Reflections on Musicians and the Difficulty of Their Role*   120

  *Outsider Concerns about the Miraculous*   121


**PART THREE: ASSISTING THE INVESTIGATION**

**Why Study Anaheim Vineyard's Worship?**

  **Suggestions for Devotional Use**   125

**Why Study Anaheim Vineyard's Worship?**

  **Discussion Questions for Small Groups**   128

**Why Study Anaheim Vineyard's Worship?**

   **A Guide for Different Disciplines and Areas of Interest**   132

Glossary   138

Suggestions for Further Study   141

Works Cited   144

Index   148

# Series Introduction

The Church at Worship offers user-friendly documentary case studies in the history of Christian worship. The series features a wide variety of examples, both prominent and obscure, from a range of continents, centuries, and Christian traditions. Whereas many historical studies of worship survey developments over time, offering readers a changing panoramic view like that offered out of an airplane window, each volume in The Church at Worship zooms in close to the surface, lingering over worship practices in a single time and place and allowing readers to sense the texture of specific worship practices in unique Christian communities. To complement books that study "the forest" of liturgical history, these volumes study "trees in the forest."

Each volume opens by orienting readers to the larger contexts of each example through a map, a timeline of events, and a summary of significant aspects of worship in the relevant time period and region. This section also includes any necessary cautions for the study of the particular case, as well as significant themes or practices to watch for while reading.

Each volume continues by focusing on the practices of worship in the specific case. This section begins with an introduction that explains the nature of participation in worship for ordinary worshipers. Many studies of worship have focused almost exclusively on what clergy do, say, and think. In contrast, insofar as historical sources allow it, this series focuses on the nature of participation of the entire community.

Each volume next presents an anthology of primary sources, presenting material according to the following categories: people and artifacts, worship setting and space, descriptions of worship, orders of worship and texts, sermons, polity documents, and theology of worship documents. Each source is introduced briefly and is accompanied by a series of explanatory notes. Inclusion of these primary sources allows readers to have direct access to the primary material that historians draw upon for their summary descriptions and comparisons of practices. These sources are presented in ways that honor both academic rigor and accessibility. Our aim is to provide the best English editions of the resources possible, along with a complete set of citations that allow researchers to find quickly the best scholarly editions. At the same time, the introductory comments, explanatory sidebars, detailed glossaries, and devotional and small-group study questions make these volumes helpful not only for scholars and students but also for congregational study groups and a variety of other interested readers.

The presentation of sources attempts, insofar as it is possible, to take into account multiple disciplines of study related to worship. Worship is inevitably a multi-sensory experience, shaped by the sounds of words and music, the sight of symbols and spaces, the taste of bread and wine, and the fragrance of particular places and objects. Worship is also shaped by a variety of sources that never appear in the event itself: scriptural commands, theological treatises, and church polity rules or guidelines. In order to help readers sense this complex interplay, the volumes in this series provide a wide variety of texts and images. We particularly hope that this approach helps students of the history of preaching, architecture, and music, among others, to more deeply understand how their interests intersect with other disciplines.

Each volume concludes with suggestions for devotional use, study questions for congregational study groups, notes for students working in a variety of complementary disciplines, a glossary, suggestions for further study, works cited, and an index.

Students of Christian worship, church history, religious studies, and social or cultural history might use these case studies to complement the bird's-eye view offered by traditional textbook surveys.

Students in more specialized disciplines — including both liberal arts humanities (e.g., architectural or music history) and the subdisciplines of practical theology (e.g., evangelism, preaching, education, and pastoral care) — may use these volumes to discern how their own topic of interest interacts with worship practices. Liturgical music, church architecture, and preaching, for example, cannot be fully understood apart from a larger context of related practices.

This series is also written for congregational study groups, adult education classes, and personal study. It may be unconventional in some contexts to plan a congregational study group around original historical documents. But there is much to commend this approach. A reflective encounter with the texture of local practices in other times and places can be a profound act of discipleship. In the words of Andrew Walls, "Never before has the Church looked so much like the great multitude whom no one can number out of every nation and tribe and people and tongue. Never before, therefore, has there been so much potentiality for mutual enrichment and self-criticism, as God causes yet more light and truth to break forth from his word."[1]

This enrichment and self-criticism happens, in part, by comparing and contrasting the practices of another community with our own. As Rowan Williams explains, "Good history makes us think again about the definition of things we thought we understood pretty well, because it engages not just with what is familiar but with what is strange. It recognizes that 'the past is a foreign country' as well as being *our* past."[2] This is possible, in part, because

---

1. Andrew Walls, *The Missionary Movement in Christian History: Studies in the Transmission of Faith* (Maryknoll, NY: Orbis Books, 1996), p. 15.

2. Rowan Williams, *Why Study the Past? The Quest for the Historical Church* (Grand Rapids: Wm. B. Eerdmans, 2005), p. 1.

of a theological conviction. As Williams points out, ". . . there is a sameness in the work of God. . . . We are not the first to walk this way; run your hand down the wood and the grain is still the same."[3] This approach turns on its head the minimalist perspective that "those who cannot remember the past are condemned to repeat it."[4] That oft-repeated truism implies that the goal of studying history is merely to avoid its mistakes. A more robust Christian sensibility is built around the conviction that the past is not just a comedy of errors but the arena in which God has acted graciously.

We pray that as you linger over this and other case studies in this series, you will be challenged and blessed through your encounter with one small part of the very large family of God. Near the end of his magisterial volume *A Secular Age,* Charles Taylor concludes, "None of us could ever grasp alone everything that is involved in our alienation from God and his action to bring us back. But there are a great many of us, scattered through history, who have had some powerful sense of some facet of this drama. Together we can live it more fully than any one of us could alone." What might this mean? For Taylor it means this: "Instead of reaching immediately for the weapons of polemic, we might better listen for a voice which we could never have assumed ourselves, whose tone might have been forever unknown to us if we hadn't *strained to understand it. . . .*"[5] We hope and pray that readers, eager to learn from worship communities across time and space, will indeed strain to understand what they find in these studies.

LESTER RUTH
*Duke Divinity School*

CARRIE STEENWYK
*Calvin Institute of Christian Worship*
*Calvin College and Calvin Theological Seminary*

JOHN D. WITVLIET
*Calvin Institute of Christian Worship*
*Calvin College and Calvin Theological Seminary*

3. Williams, *Why Study the Past?* p. 29.
4. George Santayana, *The Life of Reason* (New York: Scribner's, 1905), p. 284.
5. Charles Taylor, *A Secular Age* (Cambridge: Harvard University Press, 2007), p. 754.

# Suggestions for Complementary Reading

For students of Christian worship wanting to survey the broader landscape, we recommend using the examples of these volumes alongside other books such as Geoffrey Wainwright and Karen B. Westerfield Tucker's *Oxford History of Christian Worship* (Oxford: Oxford University Press, 2006); Gail Ramshaw's *Christian Worship: 100,000 Sundays of Symbols and Rituals* (Minneapolis: Fortress Press, 2009); Frank C. Senn's *The People's Work: A Social History of the Liturgy* (Minneapolis: Fortress Press, 2006); Martin D. Stringer's *A Sociological History of Christian Worship* (Cambridge: Cambridge University Press, 2005); James F. White's *A Brief History of Christian Worship* (Nashville: Abingdon Press, 1993); and Keith Pecklers's *Liturgy: The Illustrated History* (Mahwah, NJ: Paulist Press, 2012). A brief examination of the myriad aspects encompassing worship can be found in Juliette Day and Benjamin Gordon-Taylor's *The Study of Liturgy and Worship* (Collegeville, MN: Liturgical Press, 2013) or Ruth C. Duck's *Worship for the Whole People of God: Vital Worship for the 21st Century* (Louisville: Westminster John Knox Press, 2013).

For those studying church history, volumes from this series might accompany works such as Mark Noll's *Turning Points: Decisive Moments in the History of Christianity*, 3rd ed. (Grand Rapids: Baker Academic, 2012); Dale T. Irvin and Scott W. Sunquist's *History of the World Christian Movement*, 2 vols. (Maryknoll, NY: Orbis Books, 2001–2012); and Robert Bruce Mullin's *A Short World History of Christianity*, rev. ed. (Louisville: Westminster John Knox Press, 2014).

Students of religious studies might read these volumes alongside Robert A. Segal's *The Blackwell Companion to the Study of Religion* (Oxford: Blackwell, 2006) and Robert A. Orsi's *The Cambridge Companion to Religious Studies* (Cambridge: Cambridge University Press, 2011).

History of music classes might explore the case studies of this series with Tim Dowley's *Christian Music: A Global History* (Minneapolis: Fortress Press, 2011); Andrew Wilson-Dickson's *The Story of Christian Music: From Gregorian Chant to Black Gospel* (Minneapolis: Augsburg Fortress Press, 2003); and Suzel Ana Reiley and Jonathan M. Dueck's *Oxford Handbook of Music and World Christianities* (Oxford: Oxford University Press, 2016).

History of preaching students might study the contextual examples provided in this series along with Hughes Oliphant Old's volumes of *The Reading and Preaching of the Scriptures in the Worship of the Christian Church* (Grand Rapids: Eerdmans, 1998–2010) or O. C. Edwards's *A History of Preaching* (Nashville: Abingdon Press, 2004).

Readers interested in the broader history of contemporary worship could look at Swee Hong Lim and Lester Ruth's *Lovin' on Jesus: A Concise History of Contemporary Worship* (Nashville: Abingdon Press, forthcoming); Bryan D. Spinks's *The Worship Mall: Contemporary Responses to Contemporary Culture* (New York: Church Publishing, 2011); and Robb Redman's *The Great Worship Awakening: Singing a New Song in the Postmodern Church* (San Francisco: Jossey-Bass, 2002).

# Acknowledgments

We are grateful to the many people who have contributed to this volume. It truly has been a joint effort of many friends, some of long acquaintance and others of newly formed relationships. In particular, we offer appreciation to the following:

» the participants of this congregation, many of whom contributed new testimonies for the telling of its story and provided encouragement along the way;

» Carl Tuttle and Todd Hunter, whose conversations provided rich material for the book;

» the Wimber family for their support and assistance;

» the staffs of Vineyard USA and Vineyard Music, especially Jason Hagen for helping with copyright permissions;

» Caleb Maskell, who created an opportunity to present an earlier version of this book at a meeting of the Society of Vineyard Scholars from which we gained valuable feedback;

» the staff and student assistants at the Calvin Institute of Christian Worship, who spent countless hours copying, scanning, typing, and providing other support for this volume;

» Carrie Steenwyk and John Witvliet, co-editors for this series, who have provided both the initial vision for it as well as the ongoing impetus that makes it continue;

» Adam Perez, who checked the accuracy of citations;

» the Lilly Endowment for financial support;

» and Mary Hietbrink for assistance in the publication process.

To any who should be in this list but have been inadvertently left off, we offer both thanks and apologies.

PART ONE

# LOCATING THE WORSHIPING COMMUNITY

# The Context of the Worshiping Community: Anaheim Vineyard Fellowship, 1977–1983

Before "contemporary worship" was known by that name, what was it?

For at least one congregation, meeting in a high school gymnasium in Southern California around 1980, it was simply worship: heart-felt, life-changing, intimacy-creating, can't-wait-until-the-service-starts worship. Many of these worshipers—even (perhaps especially) the long-time church attenders—felt they truly were worshiping God for the first time in their lives. They arrived early for worship by an hour or more, eager to see how they would encounter God and poised to pour out their love to him.

They did so with songs sung lovingly to God, not just about God. A small band led; Carl Tuttle on an acoustic guitar was the chief musician. Other regular members included Dick Heying on drums, Jerry Davis on bass, and the pastor, John Wimber, on a Rhodes keyboard. Eddie Espinosa, who led worship regularly after Carl Tuttle, was also frequently one of the instrumentalists as well as a contributing songwriter. When a song required a female vocalist, Cindy Rethmeier would come forward to sing. The musicians' low, portable platform, 8 x 16 feet, seemed buried in the midst of the people. There was no set list of songs, and no lyrics were provided to the congregation.

Following the singing, the pastor, John Wimber, left his place at the keyboard to preach. His quick wit and folksy manner sprinkled his Bible-teaching sermons, making them simultaneously thoughtful and accessible. The service concluded with an opportunity for prayer. Throughout the service, Wimber might call the congregation to consider quietly how the Holy Spirit might be moving among them. The simplicity of the service's structure was mirrored in the simplicity of the space. Except for the assembly of worshiping people, no obvious symbols of Christian heritage could be seen. Nor were there any special lights or effects to heighten the drama.

The historical significance of what this congregation was doing probably went unnoticed by all. These worshipers had come to worship in a way that filled their deepest longings for **intimacy with God**. They had not come to make history.

But they—and similar congregations elsewhere—were making history. This congregation, eventually known as the Anaheim Vineyard Fellowship, was contributing to changes in Protestant worship that would come to characterize a revolution in new forms of worship in the last quarter of the twentieth century. By the 1990s these new forms would be called "contemporary worship."

This congregation, originally known as the Calvary Chapel of Yorba Linda, began meeting in a home in the mid-1970s. It launched as a congregation in May 1977. Originally part of the network of Calvary Chapels, it joined the Vineyard, a parallel network, in 1982. For the sake of clarity, the eventual name of the congregation, Anaheim Vineyard, will be used throughout this volume.

This congregation was neither the first nor the only church to be spearheading the re-shaping of worship. But its worshipers, musicians, and pastor played instrumental roles in the changes that occurred. For one thing, the Anaheim Vineyard became the mother church for a fledgling, ever-growing denomination which planted new churches aggressively around the world. With each new plant, the Vineyard way of worship spread.

Both in this congregation and throughout the denomination, music played a very central role in the development of new forms of worship. Early in its history, playing on Wimber's background in professional music, the Vineyard Fellowship began to publish and distribute new songs. Anaheim Vineyard was an environment that inspired songwriters and song leaders who were dedicated to the vision of direct, intimate interaction with God in worship songs. Some of these songs have spread around the world, and the network of Vineyard songwriters has included some of the best known composers in the contemporary worship world from the 1980s forward.

The Anaheim Vineyard's direct impact on worship spread quickly and internationally. Within just a few years of the congregation's emergence, Wimber was taking ministry teams overseas, especially to England, and shaping new expectations for encountering God in worship. The Vineyard's ministry inspired new songwriters in England whose music would eventually rebound and become widely popular in the United States in what one scholar has called the "British Invasion" into North American worship music.[1] Wimber and other Vineyard leaders led multiple conferences, classes, and other educational events that spread the Vineyard approach to worship and had a direct impact on the growing network of Vineyard fellowships and a spill-over effect across evangelical churches.

The Vineyard's impact on worship has been felt indirectly, too. Along with other churches which emerged in the 1970s, the Anaheim Vineyard helped create a new expectation in the order of worship. Rather than having isolated pieces of music embedded at points within a service, these churches began to have an extended time of music to start a service. As more and more churches adopted this approach, a sense of having a worship "set," a term appropriated from the pop music world, developed. A desire for good flow within the set naturally followed. Soon "music" and "worship" became synonymous, a new development in worship history.

Perhaps Anaheim Vineyard's most distinctive contribution to the rise of musical worship sets, which became one of the most critical features of "contemporary worship," was the emphasis upon intimacy with God in worship. The worship at Anaheim Vineyard was a direct,

Early Vineyard songs quickly traveled around the world. Some of the best-known, most influential Vineyard songwriters (and songs) in the 1980s and 1990s include Carl Tuttle ("Hosanna"); John Wimber ("Spirit Song"); Eddie Espinosa ("Change My Heart, O God"); Brian Doerksen ("Come, Now Is the Time to Worship"); Patty Kennedy-Marine ("Just Like You Promised"); David Ruis ("Worthy of My Praise"); John Barnett ("Holy and Anointed One"); Marie Barnett ("Breathe"); Andy Park ("We Exalt Your Name"); and Cindy Rethmeier ("Exalt the Lord").

1. Monique Ingalls, "Transnational Connections, Musical Meaning, and the 1990s 'British Invasion' of North American Evangelical Worship Music," in *The Oxford Handbook of Music and World Christianities*, ed. Suzel Reily and Jonathan Dueck (Oxford and New York: Oxford University Press, 2016), 425-48. For a description of Vineyard's impact on worship in England, see James Steven's "The Spirit in Contemporary Charismatic Worship," in *The Spirit in Worship—Worship in the Spirit*, ed. Teresa Berger and Bryan D. Spinks (Collegeville, MN: Liturgical Press, 2009), 245-59.

heart-felt, heart-ministering, and heart-connecting adoration of God. Anaheim Vineyard and its worship leaders were central in establishing a sense that real worship songs ought to be sung *to* the Lord, not just *about* the Lord, a sensibility that has leavened the entire contemporary worship world. Although not the only ones believing this idea, John Wimber and others from Anaheim Vineyard established this commitment as a key aspect of worship through a teaching ministry that quickly spread around the world.

Through teaching and ministry, John Wimber and the Anaheim Vineyard helped widely spread a desire for healing in worship. Wimber worked to create an expectation for finding healing and wholeness from God through worship. Always wanting to "do the stuff" (i.e., the New Testament "stuff" of miracles and healings), John Wimber and Anaheim worshipers expected the immediate work of the Holy Spirit in worship and thus popularized beliefs drawn from both Quaker and **Charismatic** sources.[2] Both then and since, however, this "Third Wave" of the Holy Spirit—as some have called it—has not been without controversy.[3]

What would one see in Anaheim Vineyard's worship? Typical services included musical worship sets, a simple order filled with simple songs sung to the Lord, an awareness of people's deepest hurts and needs, an expectation of encountering God's healing presence, a folksy and informal manner, and straightforward biblical teaching. These traits characterized Anaheim Vineyard's worship from its earliest days. And these same qualities have come to characterize much of what is known now as "contemporary worship."

But where did the Anaheim Vineyard come from? Although it would be unfair and inaccurate to say that Anaheim Vineyard was merely a product of its circumstances, it would also be inappropriate to ignore the context in which it arose. This context was a particularly unsettled one. The second half of the twentieth century was a tumultuous and a creative time in the United States, both inside and outside Christianity. As some have noted, Bob Dylan's refrain "the times they are a-changin" from the 1960s turned out to be the understatement of the decade.[4] Similarly, Love Song, one of the first Christian rock bands in the 1970s, noted a similar sense of change within the church: "It's not the way it used to be."

Indeed, the decades after World War II became a time of massive societal upheaval. As

"Charismatic" refers to a Pentecostal-type Christianity that developed in the second half of the 20th century and emphasized empowerment by the Holy Spirit.

Love Song's piece, "Little Country Church," was a commentary on Calvary Chapel Costa Mesa, which became instrumental in Southern California. The song spoke of radical changes in church life. It was recorded on The Everlastin' Living Jesus Music Concert album in 1971, the first release from Maranatha! Music.

2. For more on the Quaker perspective in the Anaheim Vineyard, see *Vineyard Roots Explained*, DVD (Yorba Linda, CA: Yorba Linda Vineyard Resource Center, 2012). On this DVD, Bob Fulton, a member of the pastor staff of Anaheim Vineyard and close friend of the Wimbers, notes the early possibility of the congregation's identification with the Foursquare Gospel Church, a Pentecostal denomination.

3. The term "third wave" is most closely associated with C. Peter Wagner, John Wimber's associate at Fuller Theological Seminary. A 1986 review of the course that Wagner team-taught with Wimber at Fuller listed some common concerns: a forgetting that God can work in the natural and ordinary; a disregard for evangelism that does not involve miraculous signs; a too-formulaic approach by which God is coerced to do human bidding; a neglecting of the social and ethical dimensions of Christian faith; and an inability to accept that not all are healed miraculously. See Ben Patterson's "Cause for Concern" in Tim Stafford, "Testing the Wine from John Wimber's Vineyard," *Christianity Today* 30, no. 11 (August 8, 1986): 20.

4. Jon Butler et al., *Religion in American Life: A Short History*, 2nd ed. (Oxford and New York: Oxford University Press, 2011), 383.

distressing as the upheaval was, it also created the space for an outpouring of creativity, which helped fuel the societal tumult. Americans, including Christians, wondered, "Will we survive? Where will we land? Is nothing sacred?" The anxiety behind these questions was sometimes felt literally as nuclear proliferation threatened the existence of the planet and spectacular shifts undercut traditional church life.

Within society a flurry of issues bombarded Americans from multiple directions. The Civil Rights Movement forced a reconsideration of race. The back of buses and separate schools became no longer accepted or acceptable. The Women's Movement and the rise of Feminism similarly caused a shift in thinking about the role of women and the relationship between the genders. The Sexual Revolution brought about its own redefinition of appropriate behavior between men and women. The spread of more accessible birth control as well as the *Roe v. Wade* court decision on abortion—depending upon moral persuasion seen as landmarks of either new liberty or immoral license—undergirded this revolution.

Various acts of violence accentuated the period's sense of dis-ease, too. Assassinations of popular politicians and public figures created a sense that social order itself could topple. Movies of fatal shots to a president's head and photos of a preacher sprawled on a motel's balcony haunted the American memory. Moreover, the nuclear standoff of the Cold War with Communism brought the prospect that the most terribly destructive instruments of war could obliterate one's entire existence. Imaginative children of the 1950s and 1960s lay in bed and wondered if their cities would be primary or secondary targets in the impending nuclear holocaust.

Even the nation's ground war with Communism, fought in the jungles and paddies of Vietnam, undercut a sense of soundness in basic institutions. Protests increased as Americans listened to the growing casualty lists on morning television. Eventually, the protests themselves proved deadly as military forces fired upon their own citizens. The vision of dead college students strewn across their campus haunted the nation.

Much residual trust in government evaporated in the aftermath of the Watergate scandal in the early 1970s. The final wave of President Richard Nixon as he left the White House, having resigned in the wake of his administration's illegal activity and lies, seemed to be a farewell, too, to the notion that even the most necessary of institutions could be trusted.

But, if the second half of the twentieth century was a tumultuous time, it was also a creative one. A flood of new creative expressions seemed to flow from cultural shifts as well as cause them. Societal change seemingly unleashed a creative impulse and, simultaneously, creativity fueled changes in the wider culture. New forms of art and architecture became common. For its eventual impact on Christian worship, the rise of pop forms of music became especially important. The creative impulse was released not just in artistic realms but also in scientific ones. Ever more startling technological advances, arriving in ever-increasing waves, marked a spirit of innovation. The time itself seemed of two minds: one moment of cultural distress was followed by another of technological wonder. These advances would eventually make their mark on Christian worship, too.

Both tumult and creativity marked American Christianity in this period, a mix which lay behind the emergence of new forms of church life and worship like Anaheim Vineyard. Some of the changes in church seemed to mirror societal revolutions directly. One example was the growing acceptance of women in ministry and the increasing number of women ordained. The novelty of seeing a woman in the pulpit was swept away within a few decades as women swelled the ranks of students in seminary and gained important positions as denominational leaders.

More broadly, other changes in churches mirrored the general tone of the times: there was a distrust of inherited institutions, a desire to create forms authentic to the people, and a reveling in the creative process itself. These sensibilities applied not only to churches where each congregation had the authority to shape its own forms of worship—the so-called Free Church Tradition—but even to the Roman Catholic Church. The Second Vatican Council in the early 1960s unleashed a torrent of liturgical experimentations and adaptations that swept across the world. Whether in Catholic parishes in Africa, Episcopal campus ministries in the American Midwest,[5] or new evangelical churches planted in Southern California, the third quarter of the twentieth century was a period when Christians became increasingly concerned that worship reflect the people and be authentic to them.

One stream of this creativity in churches was in what might be called intentional adaptation to fit the people. An example is the rise of ministry from mid-century onward targeted to different generations with their own unique situations and tastes. The result often was an adaptation of worship music to fit younger generations. As new forms of popular music arose in the decades after World War II, different groups of Christians began experimenting with new forms of worship music drawn from these secular sources. For example, the music at Youth for Christ evangelistic rallies in the late 1940s was close to the crooner, girl trio, and big-band styles of the day. But such experimentation was not limited to evangelical parachurch organizations. For instance, the 1959 Summer Convocation of Methodist Youth, meeting on the campus of Indiana's Purdue University, attracted thousands to the newly commissioned jazz setting for John Wesley's Order for Morning Prayer.[6] These examples are only a hint of the

In a 1981 *New York Times* article, Wimber noted that the Anaheim Vineyard ministered to those who questioned institutions: "We cater to the post–World War II baby boom. They are anti-institutional and don't like to be told they aren't going to church enough or giving enough." Source: Kenneth A. Briggs, "More Churches Quietly Forging Independent Paths," *The New York Times*, May 10, 1981, 26.

---

5. See Myron B. Bloy Jr., ed., *Multi-Media Worship: A Model and Nine Viewpoints* (New York: Seabury Press, 1969). For descriptions of the breadth of innovation, see Cornelius Plantinga Jr. et al., *Discerning the Spirits: A Guide to Thinking about Christian Worship Today* (Grand Rapids: Eerdmans, 2003), and Bryan D. Spinks, *The Worship Mall: Contemporary Responses to Contemporary Culture* (New York: Church Publishing Inc., 2011).

6. For a history of the particularly important example of youth ministry, see Thomas E. Bergler, *The Juvenilization of American Christianity* (Grand Rapids: Eerdmans, 2012). Bergler documents the musical aspects of teenager-targeted ministry in "'I Found My Thrill': The Youth for Christ Movement and American Congregational Singing, 1940-1970," in *Wonderful Words of Life: Hymns in American Protestant History and Theology*, ed. Richard J. Mouw and Mark A. Noll (Grand Rapids: Eerdmans, 2004), pp. 123-49. The two examples described above are from Bergler's book.

sensibility that grew into a deep commitment of the late twentieth-century church: Worship's music must fit the people who are worshiping.

Arising simultaneously with these initial explorations in worship music was a line of thinking that reinforced the rightness of intentional adaptation, the **Church Growth Movement.** Beginning with 1950s publications by Donald McGavran, a missionary to India, this approach assessed the sociological factors that accompanied people's receptivity to the Gospel and described the conditions under which churches grew. Eventually, McGavran became instrumental in organizing a School of World Mission at **Fuller Theological Seminary** in Pasadena, California, which became a center for cultivating this line of thought. From then onward, a series of books, workshops, consultations, and other promotional materials by a variety of authors reinforced a desire to find the approach to church life, including worship, which would grow a church most effectively. "Innovate or die" became a mantra for many church leaders in the late twentieth century, a commitment reinforced by growing anxieties over the numeric decline of mainline churches. In Church Growth literature, the ecclesiastical description often became ecclesiastical prescription. The perspective helped encourage the underlying cultural sensibility for intentional adaptation in worship through creativity and experimentation.

The proliferation of **megachurches**, a church with several thousands in attendance in weekly worship, in the latter half of the twentieth century has seemed to validate intentional adaptation in worship, especially to those with a Church Growth perspective. Indeed, the rise of some well-known megachurches in the 1970s and 1980s has seemed an example of the effectiveness of combining a generationally-targeted ministry with liturgical innovation. Willow Creek Community Church in Illinois, for example, grew from a youth-targeted ministry in the 1970s to one of the most influential churches by the 1990s. Such churches played a large role in spreading early forms of "contemporary worship" across American Christianity. Church leaders read the materials produced by these churches and attempted to replicate worship they experienced in their training conferences in their home congregations.

Adaptation to worship in the latter part of the century was not always an intentional, tactical decision, however. Many times creativity in new forms spontaneously arose as existing Christians had new spiritual experiences or as new groups of people came to Christian faith. In either case, the people sought to express themselves truly and authentically in worship; this expression often resulted in new forms of worship.

An important example of Christians with deepened experiences wanting to express their new piety in worship is the Charismatic Renewal Movement that spread through churches in the 1960s and 1970s. In this movement, certain classic emphases from **Pentecostalism**—which had undergone some of its own internal revitalization in the 1950s—entered many mainline churches, whether Protestant, Roman Catholic, or even Eastern Orthodox. These emphases included seeking the Holy Spirit and the Spirit's gifts, **speaking in tongues**,

As used in this volume, speaking in tongues refers to speech given supernaturally by the Holy Spirit, speech which sounds unintelligible to the human ear.

prophesying, and healing. Charismatic worship, not surprisingly, was often more demonstrative than these Christians had previously expressed. Charismatic Episcopalians, Methodists, Catholics, and Presbyterians, among others, now valued **spiritual gifts**, bodily expression, and a sense of God's immediate, active presence in worship. Moreover, charismatic Christians began to write new worship music to express their new intensity for God. The music spread across denominational lines.

Other spiritual renewal movements, like intensive retreats (e.g., the Roman Catholic Cursillo and the ecumenical Walk to Emmaus), contributed to the impulse for new ways of worship. One critical instance occurred among the hippie counterculture of California as the **Jesus Movement** surfaced in the late 1960s. Its participants, known as **Jesus People**, expressed their culture in how they worshiped, including new styles of music influenced by the pop or folk idioms. **Calvary Chapel**, under the ministry of Pastor Chuck Smith, in Costa Mesa, California, was a center of the Jesus Movement. This church embraced the worship expressions of young Californians with their zealous attention to the Bible, music influenced by pop forms, and desire for authenticity and California informality. By the early 1970s, Calvary Chapel through its music publishing arm, Maranatha! Music, and through its church-planting efforts was disseminating a new way to be church and reach people. Before long, services far removed from California's hippies were singing the choruses found on Maranatha! recordings.

Many of these creative impulses within worship, both intentional and spontaneous, lay behind the early history of the Anaheim Vineyard congregation. Even as its own musicians were beginning to craft new songs, Anaheim worshipers were singing many of the songs found on the early Maranatha! albums. That is not surprising, given that the Anaheim congregation was originally part of the Calvary Chapel network.

But the Anaheim congregation's way of worship was not merely a replication of other churches. In a special way, it synthesized much of what was developing, put its own stamp on it, and distributed it through a widespread teaching ministry by the church's leaders. For instance, Wimber's emphasis upon miraculous signs as wonders of divine power and manifestations of the Kingdom of God's in-breaking helped popularize the expectation for healing. The congregation's stress on intimacy with God in worship is another example of something that has had wide impact. Although the influence of "contemporary worship" usually is attributed to its music, the significance of Wimber's teaching ministry should not be underestimated.

In its earliest beginnings, no one would have guessed the congregation's eventual importance. The congregation began in October 1976 as a home worship group of burnt-out Christians, including many members of a **Friends** (Quaker) church in Yorba Linda, California. They met in the home of the sister of Carl Tuttle, who led the music from the praise choruses he knew.[7] The group met, prayed, and sang simple love songs to God. After a few months, the

Spiritual gifts are supernatural manifestations of the power of the Holy Spirit and the love of God. These would include prophecy, speaking in tongues, interpretation of tongues, and healings, among other gifts.

7. For a description of the worship in this home, see http://www.carltuttle.com. Accessed August 24, 2016.

husband of Carol Wimber, one of the members of the group, joined. The husband, John, had been a professional musician with The Paramours.

The Wimbers had traveled quite a path to be part of the group's renewing worship. John and Carol had been converted under the ministry of a gifted Friends Church Bible study teacher and evangelist, Lawrence "Gunner" Payne. After joining the Friends Church and quickly exhibiting strong leadership gifts, they both quickly rose in leadership at the church. By 1971, Carol was an elder in the Yorba Linda church, and John was on staff. After several years, John assumed a wider teaching role as a Church Growth consultant for an institute at Fuller Theological Seminary. But the heavy travel and demands of ministry had worn on him, too, and he followed Carol to a home meeting.

There John Wimber both received and gave. After some initial qualms over the group's songs and worship style, he experienced renewal in the group's worship and also helped provide leadership to the burgeoning fellowship. By May 1977, the group had grown so much it decided to launch publicly as a new church as part of the network that had originated with the Costa Mesa Calvary Chapel.[8] On Mother's Day that year, the fledgling congregation used a Masonic Lodge to hold its first public service as the Calvary Chapel of Yorba Linda with John Wimber as pastor.

The congregation grew quickly; it made necessary and frequent moves over its first several years as it sought out large enough worship spaces. In less than three months, by the July after their first public service, the congregation had about 200 hundred new members and already needed to move from their first worship space. In the next three months, the congregation met in Bernardo Yorba Jr. High, where they added another 250 to their number. For a year after that, they met in El Dorado High School. In that year, they added another 300 people. Following that in September 1978, they moved to Esperanza High School in Anaheim, where another 400 people joined them again within a year. From June 1979 through September 1983, the congregation added another 2,000 people to their numbers while worshiping at Canyon High School in Anaheim. Finally, in late 1983, the congregation moved to a 65,000-square-foot warehouse in Anaheim.[9]

In addition to changing location the congregation also changed its broader connections during this time; it joined other Vineyard Fellowships in 1982. The Vineyard began as a small group of churches begun in the 1970s in Southern California, led by Kenn Gulliksen, who had been interested in intimacy and freedom in worship. John Wimber's congregation joined

8. For a more detailed history, see C. P. Wagner, "Vineyard Christian Fellowship," in *The New International Dictionary of Pentecostal and Charismatic Movements*, ed. Stanley M. Burgess et al. (Grand Rapids: Zondervan, 2002), and Bill Jackson, *The Quest for the Radical Middle: A History of the Vineyard* (Cape Town: Vineyard International Publishing, 1999). For a comparative history of Calvary and Vineyard, see Donald E. Miller, *Reinventing American Protestantism: Christianity in the New Millennium* (Berkeley and Los Angeles: University of California Press, 1997). Miller's appraisal is not always sympathetic to these new movements.

9. Jackson, *The Quest for the Radical Middle,* 64.

the network in 1982, after its original association with the Calvary Chapel network dissolved because of issues dealing with Wimber's congregation's emphasis upon the Holy Spirit. Wimber soon rose to national leadership in the Vineyard.

The congregation also continued to grow dynamically as it developed its own form of worship with a dedication to new music that spoke to the Lord in loving, intimate, and simple ways with a pop sound that was familiar to the congregation's ears. The Sunday times of singing lasted between 30 minutes and 45 minutes.[10] Other key features included an interest in spiritual gifts, an informal manner of being church, and a pragmatic approach to evangelizing. Helping prepare the way for what would soon emerge as "contemporary worship," the congregation and its pastor also grew in influence around the world. History was being made.

10. See http://www.carltuttle.com. Accessed August 24, 2016.

# Timeline

| What was happening in the world? | What was happening in Christianity? | What was happening in the Anaheim Vineyard congregation? |
|---|---|---|
| | Late 1940s and early 1950s: The Pentecostal Movement, known as the Latter Rain Movement, popularizes the singing of short praise choruses. | |
| | 1954: Beginning his role as an international evangelist, Billy Graham launches a crusade in England. | |
| | 1956: *Christianity Today* begins publication. | |
| 1960: John F. Kennedy is elected President. | 1960: Dennis Bennett, an Episcopal priest in Van Nuys, California, tells his congregation that he has been baptized with the Holy Spirit. Some trace the beginning of the Charismatic Movement to this announcement. | |
| October 1962: The Cuban Missile crisis escalates. | 1962: The Second Vatican Council begins for the Roman Catholic Church and, subsequently, liturgical reform follows for several years. | |
| 1963: The first Baby Boomers turn 18 years old. | 1963: C. S. Lewis dies. | April 1963: John and Carol begin attending a Bible Study led by a Quaker, Gunner Payne. |
| November 1963: Kennedy is assassinated. | | May 1963: John and Carol become Christians. |
| 1964: Nelson Mandela, an anti-apartheid activist in South Africa, is sentenced to life in prison. | | |
| 1965: American troops begin to engage in combat in Vietnam. | | |
| 1967: The "Six-Day War" pits Israel against several neighboring nations. It ends with an Israeli victory. | 1967: The Roman Catholic charismatic renewal movement begins on college campuses. | |
| | ca. 1967–1968: The Jesus Movement, a youth-oriented counterculture emerges, especially on the West Coast. | |
| April 1968: Martin Luther King is assassinated. | | |

## What was happening in the world?

June 1968: Robert F. Kennedy is assassinated.

1968: Richard Nixon is elected President.

July 1969: The United States succeeds in landing people on the moon.

August 1969: Thousands attend the Woodstock music festival.

1970: Students at an anti-Vietnam War protest at Ohio's Kent State University are killed by National Guard troops.

1970: The rock opera *Jesus Christ Superstar* is released as a double-album.

1970: The British rock group, the Beatles, break up.

1971: Igor Stravinsky, an influential Russian composer, dies.

1972: Richard Nixon is re-elected President.

1973: The Yom Kippur War occurs among Egypt, Syria, and Israel.

1973: OPEC (Organization of the Petroleum Exporting Countries) starts an oil embargo.

1973: The last American troops leave Vietnam.

August 1974: Richard Nixon resigns as President under threat of impeachment from the Watergate scandal; Gerald Ford assumes the presidency.

1975: Bill Gates co-founds Microsoft.

1976: Martin Heidegger, an important German philosopher, dies.

1976: Jimmy Carter is elected President.

1977: The first *Star Wars* movie is released.

## What was happening in Christianity?

1968: The United Methodist Church is formed from a merger of The Methodist Church and Evangelical United Brethren.

1970: Hal Lindsey publishes *The Late Great Planet Earth.*

1971: *Time* magazine publishes an article on the Jesus Movement.

1972: Explo '72, a Christian music festival, fills the Cotton Bowl in Dallas, Texas.

1973: The National Right to Life Committee emerges from prior groups as a response to the *Roe v. Wade* Supreme Court decision regarding abortion.

1974: Maranatha! Music, associated with the Calvary Chapel in Costa Mesa, California, releases *The Praise Album.* The album includes "Seek Ye First," "Father, I Adore You," and "Glorify Thy Name."

1975: Willow Creek Community Church begins in an Illinois theater.

1977: James Dobson founds Focus on the Family.

## What was happening in the Anaheim Vineyard congregation?

1970: At the Yorba Linda Friends Church, John Wimber is very active, leading 11 Bible studies a week with over 500 people in total attendance.

1971: John Wimber joins the staff at Yorba Linda Friends Church, and his wife, Carol, is an elder in the same church.

1974: Peter Wagner offers John Wimber a job to help establish the Institute of Evangelism and Church Growth at Fuller Theological Seminary. Wimber leaves the staff of the Yorba Linda Friends Church. He directs the Institute until 1978.

1974: Coming from the Calvary Chapel in Costa Mesa, Kenn and Joanie Gulliksen move to Los Angeles to plant a church they eventually name Vineyard.

October 1976: Carol and some of the leaders of the Friends church start a home meeting. Carl Tuttle leads the music. The meeting grows from 12 to 50 in a few weeks.

April 1977: Joining the group after its start, John Wimber now leads the home meeting, which has grown to 100.

| What was happening in the world? | What was happening in Christianity? | What was happening in the Anaheim Vineyard congregation? |
|---|---|---|
| | | 1977: The Vineyard, started by the Gulliksens, continues to expand, move, and plant additional churches. |
| | | April 30, 1977: Participants in the home meeting who belong to the Yorba Linda Friends Church request a release with blessings and prayers from the group that will become Calvary Chapel of Yorba Linda; such is granted immediately. |
| | | May 1977: Wimber's group becomes the Calvary Chapel of Yorba Linda (not a Vineyard Fellowship) with 150 in attendance. (Identification with Vineyard comes later.) The congregation meets publicly in a Masonic lodge. Wimber is ordained this year by a Calvary Chapel pastor. |
| | | July 1977: The congregation moves to Bernardo Yorba Junior High School. |
| | | September 1977: The congregation moves to El Dorado High School. |
| 1978: John Paul II becomes Pope. | 1978: The *Lutheran Book of Worship* is published by a cooperative effort of several Lutheran denominations. | March 1978: Wimber and his team see their first healing after months of praying without seeing anyone cured. |
| | 1978: The Common Lectionary becomes widespread in many mainline churches. | September 1978: The congregation moves to Esperanza High School. |
| 1979: The oil crisis results from the Iranian Revolution. | 1979: The Episcopal Church (USA) publishes a new *Book of Common Prayer*, the fourth American revision since the late 18th century. | 1979: John Wimber and Kenn Gulliksen meet. |
| 1979: Margaret Thatcher becomes Prime Minister of Great Britain. | | June 1979: The congregation moves to Canyon High School, occupying the gymnasium until September 1983. |
| 1979: Mother Teresa is awarded the Nobel Peace Prize. | | Fall 1979: The first church planters, Todd and Debbie Hunter, are sent out from Wimber's church. They start their work in Wheeling, West Virginia. |
| November 1979–January 1981: The Iranian hostage crisis occurs. | | |
| 1980: Ronald Reagan is elected President. | 1980: Robert Schuller finishes building the Crystal Cathedral in Garden Grove, California. | May 1980: Visiting evangelist Lonnie Frisbee invokes the Holy Spirit, and a revival breaks out in Wimber's church. |
| | 1980: Saddleback Valley Community Church holds its first public service in Orange County, California. | |
| 1981: Diana marries Prince Charles of the United Kingdom. | 1981: Willow Creek Community Church moves to its new building in South Barrington, Illinois. | |
| 1981: The first of the space shuttles, Columbia, is launched. | | |
| 1982: *Thriller*, Michael Jackson's album, becomes the best-seller in history. | | January 1982: John Wimber team-teaches the first section of a course on Signs, Wonders, and Church Growth (MC510) at Fuller Theological Seminary. |

## What was happening in the world?

1983: U.S. Marines and Army invade Grenada.

1983: Madonna releases her debut album.

1984: Ronald Reagan is re-elected President.

1986: The space shuttle Challenger explodes after launch.

1988: George H. W. Bush is elected President.

1989: The Berlin Wall falls.

1989: The Chinese army kills thousands of pro-democracy protesters in Tiananmen Square in Beijing.

1990-1991: The United States leads an alliance to defeat Iraq in the Gulf War.

1992: Bill Clinton is elected President.

## What was happening in Christianity?

1987: Integrity Music, another publisher of contemporary worship music, is formed.

1987: Pat Robertson, host of the 700 Club, tries to become the Republican nominee for President.

1988: The Evangelical Lutheran Church in America is formed from a merger of several Lutheran churches.

1989: Christian Copyright Licensing, Inc. (CCLI) compiles its first Top 25 song list of contemporary Christian music. Pete Sanchez Jr.'s "I Exalt Thee" is #1.

## What was happening in the Anaheim Vineyard congregation?

April 1982: Calvary Chapel of Yorba Linda, the original name for Wimber's church, becomes a part of the Vineyard Fellowship.

1982: The first album, *All the Earth Shall Worship: Worship Songs of the Vineyard*, is copyrighted by Mercy Records. Wimber serves as executive producer and arranger. He also plays the keyboards.

1982: Wimber becomes head of the whole Vineyard movement.

1983: Vineyard Ministries International (VMI) is born.

September 1983: The congregation moves from a school gymnasium to a rented warehouse in Anaheim.

1986: The Association of Vineyard Churches (AVC) is incorporated.

1986: The Vineyard grows to 200 churches.

1995: John Wimber installs Carl Tuttle, the musician for the original house group, as senior pastor of the Anaheim Vineyard Christian Fellowship.

1997: A massive brain hemorrhage kills John Wimber.

1997: Lance Pittluck becomes the new senior pastor.

# Liturgical Landscape

What liturgical worlds surrounded the Anaheim Vineyard/Calvary Chapel Yorba Linda congregation? If one of this congregation's worshipers looked around Southern California, what might they see in worship?

One of the most apparent trends a worshiper would have seen was a wave of new churches—both large and small—on a parallel track to Anaheim Vineyard with respect to worship. These churches, which sociologist Donald E. Miller has called "new paradigm churches," tended to share several common characteristics: the use of pop musical instruments, songs with straightforward, simple lyrics, an extended time dedicated to congregational singing, evangelistic zeal, informality, and a commitment to biblical teaching in the sermon. One of the largest and most influential was the Calvary Chapel of Costa Mesa, California, and its network of affiliated churches. The Anaheim Vineyard was originally part of this network. The fullest documentation of Calvary Chapel is Charles E. Fromm, "Textual Communities and New Song in the Multimedia Age: The Routinization of Charisma in the Jesus Movement" (Ph.D. diss., Fuller Theological Seminary, 2006). Insider accounts can be found in Chuck Smith and Tal Brooke's *Harvest* (Costa Mesa: The Word for Today, 1987), Sharon Fischer's *I Remember . . . the Birth of Calvary Chapel* (self-published, 2014), and a DVD documentary entitled *What God Hath Wrought: Chuck Smith, the Father of the Jesus Movement* (Screen Savers Entertainment, 2012). Broader descriptions of the trend include Donald E. Miller, *Reinventing American Protestantism: Christianity in the New Millennium* (Berkeley and Los Angeles: University of California Press, 1997), and Robb Redman, *The Great Worship Awakening: Singing a New Song in the Postmodern Church* (San Francisco: Jossey-Bass, 2002). A bibliography of the Jesus Movement, one of the origins for this wave, can be found in David Di Sabatino, *The Jesus People Movement: An Annotated Bibliography and General Resource* (Lake Forest, CA: Jester Media, 2004). The best discussion of the Jesus People Movement, which lay behind many worship developments, is in Larry Eskridge, *God's Forever Family: The Jesus People Movement in America* (Oxford: Oxford University Press, 2013). Historian Michael Hamilton's article, "The Triumph of the Praise Songs: How Guitars Beat Out the Organ in the Worship Wars," in *Christianity Today* 43, no. 8 (July 12, 1999): 29–35, is a balanced look at some of the sociological reasons for the rise of these new ways of worship. Pete Ward discusses the eventual worldwide impact of these churches in *Selling Worship: How What We Sing Has Changed the Church* (Bletchley: Paternoster Press, 2005).

Influencing worship in some churches—both within and outside the "new paradigm" family—was the **Charismatic Renewal Movement**. The movement brought emphases upon the Holy Spirit, the use of spiritual gifts in worship (speaking in tongues, healing, etc.), and joyful praise, among other things. These emphases have roots in classic Pentecostal churches (e.g., Assembly of God) although they are often found in more intense or concentrated fashion in those churches. For a description of charismatic and Pentecostal worship, see Telford Work, "Pentecostal and Charismatic Worship," in *The Oxford History of Christian Worship*, ed. Geoffrey Wainwright and Karen B. Westerfield Tucker (New York: Oxford University Press, 2006), pp. 574-85. One result of the Charismatic Renewal Movement in worship was a greater value placed on an experience of the immediacy of God. A sympathetic explanation that traces that desire to Pentecostal roots can be found in David Di Sabatino, "The Unforgettable Fire: Pentecostals and the Role of Experience in Worship," *Worship Leader* 9, no. 6 (November/December 2000): 20–23.

Elsewhere in Southern California—and across the nation—there was a rise of churches adapting worship intentionally in order to attract the unchurched person. Sometimes this adaptation included adopting the worship changes of the "new paradigm churches." This pragmatic approach was often stimulated by the development of Church Growth theory among missions and evangelism experts, as occurred at Fuller Theological Seminary in Pasadena, California. This pragmatism sometimes overlapped with a charismatic perspective, but not necessarily. The approach sometimes resulted in congregations with thousands in attendance. It has occasionally been labeled a "seeker-driven" strategy. Various Southern California examples of this seeker-driven approach include the Crystal Cathedral and Saddleback Church. George G. Hunter's book, *Church for the Unchurched* (Nashville: Abingdon Press, 1996), is a sympathetic explanation of this approach's methods. The impact on worship has been described in John D. Witvliet, "The Blessing and Bane of the North American Mega-Church: Implications for Twenty-First Century Congregational Song," *Jahrbuch fur Liturgik und Hymnologie* (1998): 196–213, and Lester Ruth, "*Lex Agendi, Lex Orandi*: Toward an Understanding of Seeker Services as a New Kind of Liturgy," *Worship* 70, no. 5 (September 1996): 386–405. Todd Johnson documents the origins of many of these church's practices in youth ministry in his essay entitled "Disconnected Rituals: The Origins of the Seeker Service Movement" in *The Conviction of Things Not Seen: Worship and Ministry in the 21st Century*, ed. Todd E. Johnson (Grand Rapids: Brazos, 2002). Dave Travis and Scott Thumma's *Beyond Megachurch Myths: What We Can Learn from America's Largest Churches* (San Francisco: Jossey-Bass, 2007) is an important study of large churches.

In some of the mainline denominations, a worshiper might have seen dramatic changes taking place, especially in the revision of liturgical texts. For example, launched by the vision of the Second Vatican Council, the Roman Catholic Church was using over a century of scholarship on the history of worship to revise its liturgical books as well as to make changes in how priests led worship, in the use of the vernacular rather than Latin, in the role of laity, and in the design of the architecture, among other things. A Roman Catholic parish in 1980 usually had much different worship than it would have had in 1960. The changes are documented in both lengthy scholarly works—Annibale Bugnini, *The Reform of the Liturgy, 1948–1975*, trans. Matthew J. O'Connell (Collegeville, MN: Liturgical Press, 1990)—and in shorter historical reviews—James F. White, *Roman Catholic Worship: Trent to Today* (New York: Paulist Press, 1995). An image-driven presentation can be found in Keith F. Pecklers, *Liturgy: The Illustrated History* (Mahwah, NJ: Paulist Press, 2012).

The same liturgical history studies also brought about textual and other reforms in mainline Protestant denominations. Starting in the 1970s, Lutheran, Episcopal, Methodist, and Presbyterian churches put out new worship books. Main points of these reforms included pushing for the centrality of Christ's death and resurrection in worship content; recovering the ancient pattern of Word and Table as the standard order of worship; and encouraging full participation of the whole congregation. The changes are documented again in longer scholarly works—Frank C. Senn, *Christian Liturgy: Catholic and Evangelical* (Minneapolis: Fortress Press, 1997), especially chapter 18—and in shorter popular reviews—Robb Redman, *The Great Worship Awakening: Singing a New Song in the Postmodern Church* (San Francisco: Jossey-Bass, 2002); Thomas G. Long, *Beyond the Worship Wars: Building Vital and Faithful Worship* (Herndon, VA: The Alban Institute, 2001); and *Authentic Worship in a Changing Culture* (Grand Rapids: CRC Publications, 1997).

Probably quite apparent to a Vineyard worshiper was the type of worship most people would mean when they spoke of "traditional worship." This worship came in both "high church" and "low church" varieties and was often untouched by the sort of history-driven reforms mentioned above. Regardless of these differences in level of ceremony and formality, these churches had worship characterized by congregational singing of hymns, choirs, and a sermon that usually culminated the service. A review of the varieties of Protestant worship can be found in James F. White, *Protestant Worship: Traditions in Transition* (Louisville: Westminster/John Knox Press, 1989).

Worship across Southern California would have differed by ethnic cultures, too, even within the same denominations. Kathy Black has provided an analysis of the range one would have been likely to see across Methodism in that region in her book *Worship across Cultures: A Handbook* (Nashville: Abingdon Press, 1998). She documents distinctive practices across 21 different ethnic groups.

# Geographical Landscape

*Yorba Linda, Costa Mesa, and Anaheim are in Orange County in Southern California. Orange County is one of the most populous counties in California. It is southeast of Los Angeles. Famous for tourist attractions like Disneyland and Knott's Berry Farm, it also has been home to many large, influential churches like Robert Schuller's Crystal Cathedral (Garden Grove), Chuck Smith's Calvary Chapel (Costa Mesa), and Rick Warren's Saddleback Church (Lake Forest).*

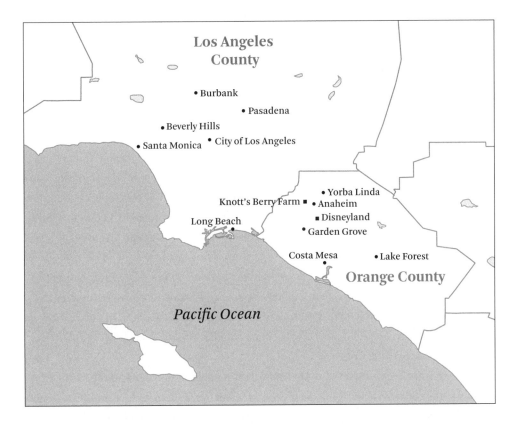

# Cautions for Studying Anaheim Vineyard's Worship History

These are some of the methodological difficulties about which a reader should be aware when reading about the Anaheim Vineyard's worship.

- Its history is not thoroughly or well documented. Only recently has this congregation, its founder, and the wider Vineyard movement become the subject of careful academic investigation. Thus, there is yet no large body of literature that has sifted through the origins and developments of Vineyard worship as with older traditions in church history.

- The scholarly literature on related movements is likewise limited, as is often the case with more recent historical phenomena, particularly those not considered mainstream or respectable at the time. Future years will see an increased discussion of Jesus People, Calvary Chapel, the Charismatic Movement, and the origins of contemporary Christian music; these discussions will help in the understanding of Vineyard history.

- Systematic collection of relevant Wimber or Vineyard documents has begun only recently with the archival collection at Regent University in Virginia Beach, Virginia.[1]

- As can be expected, the thoughts of John Wimber, the Anaheim Vineyard's founding pastor, are more systematized and more accessible after the first few years of his Vineyard ministry. This thoroughness can obscure the fresh and messy edginess of new insights. Fortunately, some of Wimber's earliest teaching on worship has been preserved by audio recording.[2]

- It is easy to forget about written documentation in exciting new movements, particularly those where spontaneity and extemporaneity are highly valued. Sometimes that means that no paper trail for later historians was created because pieces here and there that could have been helpful were discarded inadvertently. Their historical significance was not recognized at the time.

- As with other heart-emphasis approaches to Christian worship, much of the firsthand descriptions speak about personal experiences and overlook concrete details that would help later readers visualize a whole service. Thus, nuts-and-bolts issues like orders of worship and use of the space are harder to document.

- The historiography (the writing and interpreting of history) of the Vineyard Fellowship

---

1. See http://www.regent.edu/lib/special-collections/wimber-collection.cfm. Accessed August 24, 2016.
2. At the time of this publication, several resources are available on YouTube.

is still wrapped up with the personality and ministry of John Wimber. Consequently, the influence of other leaders, like Carol Wimber, Carl Tuttle, and Kenn Gulliksen, is harder to assess.

- As with any congregation's worship, the actual sound and feel cannot be reproduced simply by describing them on paper. This deficiency is especially the case in a church like the Anaheim Vineyard, where music, with its feel and rhythms, was such an important part of the experience. The full portrayal of a congregation's worship is limited by the medium of reading and writing.

# Significant Themes and Practices to Observe

In the material on Anaheim Vineyard, be on the lookout for these significant themes and practices that are categorized by some of the primary elements in the practice of worship.

## Piety

- Jesus Christ was often the focus of worship, not only as the mediator of worship to God the Father, but also as the object of worship. Thus, when the "worship of God" is mentioned, often what is understood is the worship of Jesus Christ.
- This attachment to Jesus was expressed in strong terms of personal relationship.
- Intimate communion with God was the desired end of worship, particularly in the opening musical segment. The music was often what was meant by "worship" in this church. Intimacy involved a vivid sense of knowing God's acceptance and closeness as well as feeling as if one was involved in active interaction with God or Jesus.
- Expressing love toward God was seen as "ministering to the heart of God." Likewise, in worship, God touched worshipers' hearts and lives with a ministry of love, power, and healing.
- Reflecting the expectations of the Charismatic Movement, this church desired the Holy Spirit to be active in its worship. The Spirit's activity was occasionally seen in demonstrations of spiritual gifts, especially healing.
- At times, when they felt led by the Holy Spirit, people could be physically expressive in worship, including the raising of hands.
- In addition to community worship services, "worship" was also defined by a faithfulness to living as disciples of Christ on a day-to-day basis.
- The Quaker background of many of the early participants, including its pastor and lead musician, also represents values by which worship was led, especially direct dependence upon the Holy Spirit to discern what to do next.

## Time

- Keeping a detailed liturgical calendar of special weekly and annual celebrations was not important. More emphasis was placed on worshipers' hearts than on keeping strict rhythms of time.
- The congregation worshiped on Sunday mornings and evenings.
- Small group meetings in homes supplemented the meetings for the entire congregation.

## Place

- The emphasis upon the engagement of the worshiper's heart with God seems reflected in the preference for simple worship spaces.
- The congregation began in a home setting where intimacy, comfort, informality, hospitality, and strong people dynamics were natural. These values carried over as the congregation moved to more public settings for worship.
- The rapid growth of the congregation caused multiple moves in the first several years.
- Before building any permanent home, the congregation worshiped in a series of school gymnasiums.
- The layout used in the gymnasiums put the musicians on the same floor level, only elevated by a slight platform, as most of the congregation. The platform placed the musicians very close to the people, without much separation.
- Preaching took place on the same platform, too. Again, the preacher was very close to the people.

## Prayer

- The congregation did not use written prayer texts (except for song texts, which were neither projected nor distributed on paper).
- Reflecting the long history of Protestant, heart-oriented worship traditions, the congregation valued extemporaneous prayers that were authentic and heartfelt.
- An extended time of ministering to people by prayer often ended worship services. Thus services often had a three-part order: sung worship, preaching, and prayer ministry.
- Praying for people's healing was an especially important part of the church's prayer ministry. This approach was anchored in John Wimber's emphasis upon "**power evangelism**" through which people would encounter the power of the God of the Gospel seen

through "**signs and wonders**," a shorthand way by which Wimber and others referred to supernatural manifestations given by the Holy Spirit.

- The emphasis on God's power was more than a demonstration of cold, uncaring power. The congregation expressed its deep concerns for people and their deeply felt needs—and thus the love of God—by interceding for them.

## Preaching

- John Wimber's winsome nature, accessible speech, and ease with the Bible were an attractive combination.
- The preaching had a strong element of teaching as Wimber sought to ground the congregation's practices—including its worship—in biblical explanation.
- Preaching in worship services was supplemented by other opportunities to be taught biblical doctrine, such as conferences.
- The need for teaching was due to a large influx of new people. Many had no Christian background while others came from churches that had been different from the Vineyard Fellowship.

## Music

- From its first days as a house meeting, strong congregational singing with lyrics that touched the heart was a defining element for this church.
- "Worship" was often synonymous with the extended time of congregational singing at the beginning of the services.
- The hope for these musical sets was an ever-increasing sense of intimate, loving communion with God. Expectations for experiencing God's presence in worship could become attached to the music as the mediator of that experience.
- Many of the first participants felt dissatisfied with older church music that seemed to have been sung more *about* God than *to* God. Therefore, this congregation valued songs that allowed them to speak directly to God in love.
- In both instrumentation and lyrics, this congregation's worship music reflected larger changes going on in many churches in Southern California.
- The simple and repetitive lyrics allowed the worshiper to go beyond the words to a deeper, fuller engagement with God.
- The Vineyard way of worship seems to have sparked a creative impulse to write new songs, then and now. Drawing upon his background as a professional musician, Wimber

could provide guidance for wider publication of these efforts. The resulting companies, Vineyard Ministries International and Vineyard Music, grew into major distributors of "contemporary" worship music.

## *People*

- New Christian movements across California in the 1960s and 1970s anticipated the start of this congregation. The Jesus People Movement and the Calvary Chapel of Costa Mesa were particularly influential.
- That the congregation was called the Vineyard *Fellowship*, not the Vineyard *Church*, should indicate how important personal relationships were. Pastoral care was not reserved for a class of clergy or staff; rather, the whole congregation participated in ministering to the needs of people. This approach is often typical for groups with a strong emphasis upon the Holy Spirit in their midst. The spiritual gifts mentioned in the Bible were not limited to clergy.
- A strong sense of belonging to one another was created by small groups, called **Kinship groups**, meeting in homes.
- Friends inviting friends was an important part of the explosive numeric growth of the congregation.
- The laid-back, informal style of Southern California culture influenced how the congregation conducted itself in worship. Informal dress was one example.
- Pictures of this early congregation seem to indicate a very young, White demographic; many worshipers were baby boomers.

# PART TWO

# EXPLORING THE WORSHIPING COMMUNITY

# Describing the Community's Worship: Questions and Answers with Andy Park

*What follows is a description of how the Anaheim Vineyard congregation worshiped in the late 1970s and early 1980s. This account focuses on its origins and the influence of its pastor, John Wimber. These descriptions provided by a worship leader and songwriter with a long connection to the Vineyard movement offer useful background information and perspective for this congregation's worship.*

*As a theological introduction, it interprets this history as God's activity and uses terms and categories important to the rise of the Vineyard movement. In this way the author conveys a sense of the experience of the early Vineyard worshipers as they felt the activity of God in their midst.*

## *What was worship like at the Anaheim Vineyard Fellowship in the early 1980s?*

Worship at Anaheim Vineyard Fellowship was based on the simple act of coming to God honestly and without pretense. Much of the time, such worshipful surrender was expressed by listening to God and silently meditating on God's goodness. Worshipers were taught that worship in the Bible included a wide spectrum of expressions. If giving oneself to God led to exuberance, that was wonderful. If it led to weeping, that was welcome, too, since crying and repenting, when inspired by the Holy Spirit, was seen as an act of worship. Indeed, Anaheim Vineyard worshipers believed God would give them a gift of repentance, to which the best response was to agree with what God was doing. For many, the sense of vulnerability to God, both holy and loving, led to a deep sense of conviction in worship and outward signs of repentance. In this fledgling congregation, the proper response to God was not to maintain decorum, control, and respectability, but to give oneself completely to God.

The following are memories of worship from this time from various worshipers within the Anaheim Vineyard congregation:

> I came into the gym and sat down and was quite overwhelmed by the natural, down-to-earth experience that was different from any church I had been to before. When John Wimber sat at the piano and played the first chord, I immediately started crying, and felt a presence that was so overwhelming, I realized this must be the Holy Spirit (duh), and I experienced an intimacy [with God] that I had not before. I felt like the words were piercing my heart, and I realized I

was experiencing love, grace, mercy and God himself was there with me. I suddenly realized that worship was an experience between me and God, and in this case music was the tool in which he was meeting me.[1]

The words and the music were simple, but the impact of God's Spirit touching everyone in that room was incredible. From expressions of sheer joy to tears, people lifted hands high fully abandoned and without embarrassment. I remember thinking how intimate and personal this experience was. And at the same time how pleasing this was to God. The memories of those early days will never leave me, and the impact of those times changed my view on worship forever. Worship was not just a part of a Sunday service but the entry gate to intimacy with God. Worship was a place to enter in, a place where everything starts. God was moving again in his church through worship and teaching all of us what it meant to truly seek him through the act of worship.[2]

At that time [during the early days of worship renewal], I began having wonderful times of prayer, experiencing repentance and renewal in my adoration of Jesus.[3]

The songs were dynamic, heartrending, thrilling, and I could never sing without weeping and yearning for God. . . . It was the best of times back then.[4]

The transforming power of Vineyard worship was so much more than words, notes, or even musical performance; it was the intervention of the Holy Spirit. The Holy Spirit brought a tangible knowledge of God on a deep heart level and a hunger to know God much more. If the Anaheim Vineyard congregation aspired to anything in worship, it was for people's hearts to be near to God. Worshipers saw spiritual intimacy with God in the revival of conversions and spiritual gifts they experienced at Anaheim Vineyard. According to Todd Hunter, former Vineyard church planter and assistant to Wimber in the Association of Vineyard Churches, Vineyard worship had three distinguishing characteristics: "intimacy with God, the manifest presence of the Holy Spirit, and a culture of expecting God to visit his church powerfully in every time of worship."[5] These characteristics created a unique worship experience at the Anaheim Vineyard congregation.

John Wimber, the Anaheim Vineyard pastor, was fond of quoting the late 19th-century Anglican Archbishop of Canterbury, William Temple, who said, "To worship is to quicken

---

1. Char Turrigiano, electronic mail to Cindy Rethmeier, May 19, 2006.
2. Chris DeWitt, electronic mail to Cindy Rethmeier, May 21, 2006.
3. Penny Fulton, electronic mail to Cindy Rethmeier, May 20, 2006.
4. Mary Guleserian, electronic mail to Cindy Rethmeier, May 21, 2006.
5. Andy Park, *The Worship Journey: A Quest of Heart, Mind, and Strength* (Woodinville, WA: Augustus Ink Books, 2010), 86.

the conscience by the holiness of God, to feed the mind with the truth of God, to purge the imagination by the beauty of God, to open the heart to the love of God and to devote the will to the purpose of God."[6] Wimber continually emphasized this broad definition of worship. He would often say, "Every act of obedience is worship. Every time we choose another over ourselves, it is an act of worship. Every time we decide to lay our own way down in favor of Jesus' way is an act of worship."[7] For the Anaheim Vineyard congregation, the vision of worship as all of life not only focused their corporate times of worship but shaped their personal lives as well.

## How did the name and location of the church change over the years?

The name and location of the church varied over the first several years as the congregation experienced phenomenal growth and changed facilities numerous times. Beginning in a home, the congregation used the following public spaces: a Masonic Lodge in Yorba Linda (5/77–7/77) with 200 person growth, Bernardo Yorba Jr. High in Yorba Linda (7/77–9/77) with 250 person growth, El Dorado High School in Placentia (9/77–9/78) with 300 person growth, Esperanza High School in Anaheim (9/78–6/79) with 400 person growth, and Canyon High School in Anaheim (6/79–9/83) with 2,000 person growth.[8] In late 1983, the congregation moved to a 65,000 square foot warehouse in Anaheim.

Although the congregation was originally associated with the network of Calvary Chapels, it eventually became known as Anaheim Vineyard. This congregation did not, however, start the Vineyard movement. A small group of churches, begun in the 1970s and led by Kenn Gulliksen, had been known as the Vineyard prior to Wimber's congregation joining the movement in 1982. After it joined, Wimber's congregation was a major part of the Vineyard, and Wimber himself the strongest leader. Wimber and his congregation dissolved the original association with the Calvary Chapel movement because of issues dealing with the Holy Spirit and Church Growth principles. Through the 1980s both movements grew exponentially. Eventually the Vineyard would organize national and international administrative and publishing structures.

6. John Wimber, "The Life-Changing Power of Worship," in *All About Worship: Insights and Perspectives on Worship*, ed. Julie Bogart (Anaheim, CA: Vineyard Music Group, 1998), 7.

7. John Wimber, *The Way In Is the Way On* (Atlanta: Ampelon Publishing, 2006), 114.

8. Bill Jackson, *The Quest for the Radical Middle: A History of the Vineyard* (Cape Town: Vineyard International Publishing, 1999), 64.

## *What role did Wimber have in the formation of the Anaheim Vineyard Fellowship?*

Much of the history and character of the Anaheim Vineyard is wrapped up with John Wimber and his background. Understanding his journey provides insight into the congregation's worship. In addition, many of the first members shared similar background and concerns about what they had previously experienced in worship.[9]

Before working in the Anaheim Vineyard, the Holy Spirit began working in the life of its leader. God prepared a man named John Wimber. John would say he was raised in a "pagan" home. He grew up in Missouri, in a family he described as dysfunctional. He never really knew his father, and he was exposed to lots of alcoholism as a child. He began to play the saxophone and many other instruments as a child and played professionally as a teenager. Later he went on to such notable musical accomplishments as musical director of the popular group, the Righteous Brothers.

John Wimber was converted to Christ in his late twenties after a short but successful career as a music producer and performer. A spiritual awakening came his way. In 1963, his wife, Carol began attending a Bible study. John tagged along and so met Gunner Payne, from the Friends Church (Quaker). Payne was a gifted evangelist. Before too long, John Wimber found himself on his knees, confessing his sin to God and receiving Christ. After his conversion, Wimber left his professional music career behind as he pursued ministry more and more. As it was for Payne, evangelism was always a priority for Wimber's ministry. Wimber would go on to personally lead thousands of people to Christ, and, years later, evangelism would become an important part of Anaheim Vineyard's mission.

Wimber's first experience in congregational ministry began when he joined the staff of a Friends church in Southern California in 1971. This Quaker shaping of his thought is often overlooked today, but it seems to have affected Wimber's approach to worship. The classic Friends' tradition highly valued waiting on the Lord in the context of a group. Listening to God and responding to the spontaneous initiative of God were key themes in these meetings. This approach shaped John Wimber's experience of worship. Much of early Anaheim Vineyard worship, like Wimber's experience with the Friends, was meditative and gentle with

Not surprisingly, Wimber's love of music affected his leadership as a pastor. He didn't just preach; he also led worship by playing an instrument and leading congregational singing. Consequently, music became an important part of Vineyard worship.

Carl Tuttle, the congregation's worship leader, notes the following Quaker values shaping the congregation's worship and his leadership of it: simplicity, intimacy, accessibility, lack of hype, submission, non-manufactured reverence, and a hunger and thirst to meet with God. Source: Carl Tuttle, email message to Lester Ruth, February 2, 2013.

9. Don Williams, a long-time Vineyard pastor (Ph.D. from Columbia University) who is a well-respected voice among Vineyard circles, has written about Wimber's influence: "The theological story of the Vineyard is, in its first phase, also the story of John Wimber, one of the outstanding church leaders of the last quarter of the 20th century." Williams bases his opinion in part on the accolades others have showered on Wimber, noting, "Robert Schuller, TV pastor of the Crystal Cathedral, calls him 'one of the twelve most influential Christian leaders of the last two decades.' Peter Wagner, formerly of Fuller Theological Seminary, believes that 'John was one of those extremely rare people who will be remembered as a molder of an entire generation.' Anglican Bishop David Pytches holds that Wimber has had the greatest impact on the church in England since John Wesley." Source: Don Williams, "Historical-Theological Perspective and Reflection on John Wimber and the Vineyard," http://vineyardindonesia.org/index.php?option=com_content&view=article&id=45%3Aborneo&catid=1%3Alatest&showall=1. Accessed July 4, 2008, January 16, 2013, and August 24, 2016.

an emphasis on hearing from God and communing quietly with him. This theology of God's transforming power in daily life was a guiding principle affecting every aspect of worship, on Sundays and in all other settings throughout the week.

By 1976, John Wimber was burned out from many years of hard ministry at home and on the road. He and his wife Carol resigned from their position at the Friends church but felt desperately in need of God's touch. At that time, the Wimbers—first Carol and then John—joined a group that included former Quaker acquaintances. The group often worshiped, singing love songs to Jesus, for one to two hours. One of the hallmarks of Vineyard worship, the extended times of worship, was thus set in place. Realizing the importance of this music and being comfortable using it was not necessarily an easy step for John Wimber. He describes his first exposure to this new model of worship:

I took my seat on the couch a few minutes late. When I looked around the softly lit living room, no one looked back. Eyes were closed, postures relaxed. A few were seated, some knelt and two women stood with their hands turned upward. The guitar strummed softly and played the same three chords over and over again as each member of this little gathering in Yorba Linda, California, sang to the Lord. They seemed to sing forever. *What was the point?* I thought. *Weren't we there to study the Bible?* I felt the heat rise in my cheeks; my palms became sweaty; I was embarrassed by the intimate language of these songs. "Lord, am I supposed to sing to you like that too?" I certainly hoped not! Yet within a few weeks, I felt my heart soften. I was caught off guard by the power of the lyrics in those songs. Tears rolled down my cheeks as the music played. My mind couldn't comprehend what my heart was experiencing. Singing those sweet simple love songs to the Lord led me into personal revival. Intimate worship transformed my life as a Christian. In fact, what I experienced in this small group became the foundation for the Vineyard movement.[10]

In this home group, Wimber began to exercise his gift for leadership, and the group grew. Taking leave from the elders in the Friends church, a new church was launched publicly with services on Mother's Day, May 8, 1977. The new congregation, at first affiliated with Calvary Chapel,[11] a California church that had utilized alternative forms of popular music in worship to connect with people, including Hippies and Jesus People, who were often left out of traditional churches. This new church congregation was originally known as Calvary Chapel

---

10. Wimber, *The Way In Is the Way On*, 111-12.

11. See C. P. Wagner, "Vineyard Christian Fellowship," in *The New International Dictionary of Pentecostal and Charismatic Movements*, ed. Stanley M. Burgess et al. (Grand Rapids: Zondervan, 2002), 1177. For a more detailed history, see Jackson, *The Quest for the Radical Middle*. For a comparative history of Calvary and Vineyard, see Donald E. Miller, *Reinventing American Protestantism: Christianity in the New Millennium* (Berkeley and Los Angeles: University of California Press, 1997). Miller's appraisal is not always sympathetic to these new movements.

Yorba Linda. Wimber and Calvary Chapel eventually parted ways in the early 1980s, partly over Wimber's increasing emphasis upon people being able to experience the power of the Kingdom of God today.

Working closely with his wife, Carol, and a cadre of like-minded Californians, Wimber sought to explore a way of worship where people hungering for God could experience knowing him on a deep heart level by the power of the Holy Spirit. God surprised this group of burned-out Christians with his powerful presence as they met to worship in a church member's living room.

## What were some characteristics of early worship in this congregation?

As founding pastor and a strong, articulate leader, Wimber's character and theology deeply influenced the nature of the fledgling congregation. Much of Anaheim Vineyard's initial history is deeply woven with him, and his experiences had a major influence on how this Vineyard congregation worshiped. For example, because he grew up outside the church, Wimber easily thought about ways of experiencing God in worship that went beyond the bounds of staid, traditional liturgy. His goal was always intimacy with God and vulnerability to him. This intimacy could engage a range of feelings and emotions, bringing about a wide spectrum of expressions. But emotions were never the focal point of worship. While some experienced an outpouring of emotion, many others were quietly waiting on God and feeling very little.

Given the importance of music in the Vineyard's way of worship, it would have been easy for music and musicians to become the actual center of worship, not God. But John Wimber was aware of this danger and worked to avoid it, as I (Andy Park) have noted elsewhere:

> One of the biggest things that stands out in my mind about John Wimber's heart for worship is the way he jealously guarded God's glory. Coming from the music industry, John had been around all sorts of self-promoting musicians. He was very sensitive to the issue of showmanship versus worship. Worship music was to be Christ-centered, not man-centered.
>
> Whenever the focus became the music rather than the Lord, it made John uncomfortable. He strongly valued the activity of the Holy Spirit in the midst of worship, and the importance of being sensitive to God. John always led us to come to worship with an expectation to meet with God rather than putting on a show.[12]

Worshipers found that God would cut through the tough religious exterior of committed Christians who had been hardened through life and prior church experiences. God would

---

12. Wimber, *The Way In Is the Way On,* 105.

extend, as one early worshiper, Penny Fulton, described it, a simple grace-filled message: "Come to me, lay your burdens down . . . seek me as your Lord, your portion, your treasure . . . let me love you."[13] Many early accounts of Anaheim Vineyard worship emphasized the wooing, drawing, and convicting work of the Holy Spirit as God came near to his people in worship.

Whether letting God have all of one's self led to joy or weeping or stillness, this congregation wanted worship to engage the whole worshiper. Another key characteristic of early Vineyard worship, then, was that one's entire body and spirit were involved. Carol Wimber, John's wife, once noted:

> Worship involves not only our thought and intellect, but also our body. The Scriptures are packed with a dizzying variety of praise expressions including singing, playing instruments, dancing, kneeling, bowing down, raising our hands, and so on. These are all aspects of true worship.[14]

Jesus People worship God in the late 1960s or early 1970s.

Source: Ronald M. Enroth et al., *The Jesus People* (Grand Rapids: Eerdmans, 1972), 9. Used with permission.

13. Penny Fulton, electronic mail to Cindy Rethmeier, May 20, 2006.
14. Wimber, *The Way In Is the Way On,* 119.

Wimber taught that worship is not only cognitive exchange between God and us, but it is also "trans-rational" in that it goes far beyond the realm of the human mind. ("Trans-rational" was a favorite Wimber term.) Communion with God involves the human spirit engaging with God's Spirit. To illustrate this, Wimber said, "Worship is more easily caught than taught." He applied that catchy phrase to other Spirit-inspired activities, such as praying for the sick. By this he meant being around people who are worshiping teaches others how to worship.[15]

Addressing God directly was a high priority for the congregation. For instance, John Wimber emphasized singing songs *to* God, not just *about* him. During the earliest days of the first Anaheim Vineyard group, worshipers noticed the strong presence of God during many of the songs sung in the first (I) and second (You) person directly to the Lord. While they sang some songs describing God (referring to God in the third person), they also wanted to open their hearts to him, as Carol Wimber recalls: "Worship was perhaps the first thing God told us to do and then He had to teach us how. . . . This was revolutionary to us: singing songs straight to Jesus. We sang love songs to Jesus, and it was this intimacy that broke us down."[16] Carol Wimber describes the difference between staying at a distance from God by singing *about* him compared to singing *to* him:

> You can still keep a certain reserve intact singing theological songs about the faith. These songs are wonderful and I'm thankful for every one of them. But when you sing "You Bless Me Lord Forever" or "Whom Have I But You?" it breaks through to your inner being, and expresses what your spirit needs to say.[17]

This kind of intimate worship developed a culture of expectancy in the Anaheim Vineyard. These deep experiences of God's presence and activity in worship had people eagerly anticipating each weekly gathering. Having experienced a closeness to God that was so satisfying and having seen God move in their midst time and again, worshipers arrived each week excited to see what God might do on that Sunday. Todd Hunter, one of the early participants, described their expectancy:

> We literally could not wait to get to church, to be in the congregation, to worship, to see what God would do today, etc. We felt anticipation and we had legitimate hope that God would visit us in worship because he was consistent in doing so. . . . I don't ever remember anyone walking out of the gym and remarking about the band, the great guitar licks, the cool piano chops or

15. For more on this, see Andy Park's *To Know You More: Cultivating the Heart of the Worship Leader* (Downers Grove, IL: InterVarsity Press, 2002), 211-14.

16. Wimber, *The Way In Is the Way On*, 108.

17. Wimber, *The Way In Is the Way On*, 108.

the amazing vocal performances. It was all about feeling and knowing the presence of God and responding to him in worship.[18]

Often when God visited, he healed. And thus, an expectation for healing became a common part of worship. Consequently, services often included a time for prayer on people's behalf, usually at the end of the service. Wimber notes the connection between worship and healing in the congregation's origins: "One of the first things God taught us was the value of worship. In those early days, worship became vital to us. It was all we could do. We were so weak and sick ourselves we had nothing to offer Him except our praise. As we worshiped God, we began to get well."[19]

## What was unique about the opening set of songs?

Worship was the first priority of the church. The church spent large portions of time learning to express its love to God in—to use Wimber's phrasing—"intimate, loving and adoring language." Wimber compared worship to an intimate, two-way conversation between a married couple. Over dinner, the pair has a long, leisurely conversation that deepens as the evening progresses. They sit face to face, speaking and listening to one another. Relationship is deepened through time spent together. Thus, Sunday meetings typically began with 30 to 45 minutes of uninterrupted singing. Just as a married couple goes out to dinner to dedicate time to being together without interruption from the kids, the church would set aside announcements and teaching for a period in order to commune with God in sung adoration and thanksgiving.

Sunday services at the Anaheim Vineyard usually began with this extended time of worship. Initially, in the late 1970s and early 1980s, Carl Tuttle led worship with no song set list but by immediate, active listening to the Spirit's leadership. As the pastor, John Wimber, and the music leaders saw how God often worked in worship (i.e., the music set), they also observed a progression of heart attitudes and responses to God as the worship unfolded from beginning to end. This progression often became a kind of order for the opening worship. Wimber intended for the model to be descriptive, not prescriptive; it did not determine all worship planning and leading. But this progression frequently was the way the thirty- to forty-five-minute worship set developed. Songs were selected according to their appropriateness for each of the progression's phases.

The goal, regardless of phase, always remained intimacy with God. (See pp. 103, 107 to see Wimber's teaching on this directly.) The first phase was a call to worship. As an invitation

In terms of active listening to the Spirit's leadership in worship, consider this classic statement of a Quaker approach to worship: "All true and acceptable worship to God is offered in the inward and immediate moving and drawing of his own Spirit, . . . when assembled, the great work of one and all [worshipers] ought to be to wait upon God and, returning out of their own thoughts and imaginations, to feel the Lord's presence, and know a gathering into his name indeed, where he is in the midst [of the people], according to his promise." Source: Robert Barclay, "Proposition XI," *An Apology for the True Christian Divinity*, 1678 A.D.

18. Todd Hunter, electronic mail to Cindy Rethmeier, May 20, 2006.
19. John Wimber, "Zip to 3,000 in 5 Years," *Christian Life* 44, no. 6 (October 1982): 21.

The Anaheim Vineyard congregation sings in the Canyon High School gymnasium.

Source: Back cover of the 1982 album entitled *All the Earth Shall Worship: Worship Songs of the Vineyard* (Mercy Records). Used with permission.

to worship, the call could be directed either toward the people or toward God. The second phase was engagement. At this point, the songs and prayers opened up the congregation's hearts in an "electrifying dynamic of connection to God and to each other."[20] A full range of prayer (love, adoration, praise, jubilation, intercession, and petition) could be involved. The third phase involved moving into more loving and intimate language. The sense of being in God's presence was heightened and the sense of closeness with God was most intense during the third phase. During this time the music could help worshipers express their deepest love to God for his deeds, character, and attributes. In a similar way worshipers were to engage in ministry to each other as the Spirit led. Prayer and healing were not simply the work of the clergy or staff; they were the work of all worshipers under the Spirit's guidance.

The fourth phase of the progression was the worshipers' expression in worship, which could include spiritual gifts like dance or **prophecy** (the Holy Spirit gives a message to an individual to deliver to others). Having the Spirit's guidance to move was important since it was considered inappropriate for worshipers to stir themselves up to express something, as noted by Wimber: "This (physical and emotional expression) is an appropriate response to God if

An expectation for the Spirit's work through all the people in worship is another point of connection with the congregation's Quaker roots. Who in your church is expected to minister during worship? Clergy? Musicians? Everyone?

20. John Wimber, "Worship: Intimacy with God," in *Thoughts on Worship* (Anaheim, CA: Vineyard Music Group, 1996), 4.

the church is on that crest. It is most inappropriate if it is whipped up or if the focal point is on the dance rather than on the true jubilation in the Lord. . . . When we cultivate stillness as a part of our worship time together, we are enriched by the deep communion that can take place."[21] A time of visitation from God often followed. Worshipers should wait and be attentive to see how God might move at this point.[22] Dance and other expressions were not to bring attention to worshipers but to the Lord. In the fourth phase, the congregation was to wait and see how God would speak, move, or act through the Holy Spirit. Drawing people away from their preoccupations and concerns, the point of the musical set was to gather them expectantly before a God who still eagerly desired to minister among his people.

The fifth phase of worship, which came after the service itself, involved mirroring God's own graciousness in the world, expressed in whole-hearted giving to God and others in daily life. This "giving of substance" was to be the essence of a life lived as a worship ministry before God. This sense helps keep worship from being self-centered and self-absorbed as the worshiper feels the call to give to others. Seeking to give to God and others not only in a worship service but as a way of life was how worship could become all-encompassing.[23] Wimber himself was eager to point out this dimension early in the congregation's history as he said in 1982: "Recently God led us to take a new step in our development: We began to care for the poor in earnest."[24]

Worshipers also gathered in small groups during the week to practice and develop their spiritual gifts. Beyond the Sunday worship, worshipers gathered in homes as "Kinship groups." These were safe places where people could learn to move in the Spirit as they sensed the Lord's anointing.

## What was the role of spiritual gifts and healing?

In the late 1970s, as the new congregation was being established, Wimber also began to reconsider an earlier reluctance about seeing the gifts of the Holy Spirit as still operating in the church. Specifically, Wimber began to look for the possibility of seeing healings and other dramatic movements of the Spirit in worship. Wimber was drawn to the stories of church growth accompanied by miracles told by missionaries he had met while he worked at Fuller Theological Seminary in Pasadena, California, as a Church Growth consultant.

Several factors reinforced the affirmation of modern-day miracles. For one thing, Peter

---

21. Wimber, *The Way In Is the Way On*, 122-23. See also Wimber, "Worship: Intimacy with God," 5.
22. For more on the Quaker connection to this sensibility, listen to the interview of Carol Wimber and Bob and Penny Fulton on *Vineyard Roots Explained* (Yorba Linda, CA: Yorba Linda Vineyard Resource Center, 2012), DVD.
23. Wimber, "Worship: Intimacy with God," 4-7. See also Wimber, *The Way In Is the Way On*, 121-24.
24. Wimber, "Zip to 3,000 in 5 Years," 22.

Wagner, another Fuller professor, was also going through a similar shift in his worldview. Wagner and Wimber both began to realize that their anti-supernatural stance had been based more in a modernistic worldview than the study of Scripture. Wimber began to read the kingdom theology of George Ladd, which gave him the exegetical foundation for the ongoing ministry of the Spirit in the church.[25] In addition, John and Carol had also been attending one of the churches affiliated with the Calvary Chapel movement where the teaching of Pastor Chuck Smith on the ministry of the Spirit was practical and timely.

The Anaheim Vineyard congregation began to study spiritual gifts, and Wimber began to teach on the subject of healing from the Gospel of Luke. (To see Wimber's acknowledgement of spiritual gifts in the late 1970s, see p. 97.) "After teaching on healing for nine months and seeing no one healed, they were ready to quit. God gave Wimber an ultimatum: either teach on healing or leave the ministry. Wimber chose to stay and teach, and before the tenth month they saw their first person healed. From that point the healings began to trickle, then pour in."[26] The lasting result on Vineyard worship was a commitment to give time in the service to pray for healing.

> While all this had been happening, one could not say that their church was dramatically "charismatic." There were no intense outbreaks of tongues or other overt manifestations of the Spirit—that is, until May of 1980. Wimber asked a young man converted during the Jesus People movement named Lonnie Frisbee to give his testimony.[27] After finishing, Frisbee invited all the people twenty-five years old and younger to come forward. He then invited the Holy Spirit to bring God's power. What happened is now legendary in Vineyard folklore. The young people were filled with the Spirit, began to fall over, speak in tongues, and shake. Witnesses said it looked like a battlefield. . . . Those young people, many of them junior high and high school age, were so lit on fire for God that they began to see their friends healed and brought to Christ from all over town. . . . Within months, Wimber's church had catapulted into rapid growth, launching what he would later come to call "power evangelism" i.e., conversions precipitated by healings and miracles.[28]

25. Jackson, *The Quest for the Radical Middle,* 54, 112. For a review of the conservative evangelical critiques sometimes made of Wimber and responses to them, see Joseph T. Zichterman, "The Distinctives of John Wimber's Theology and Practice within the American Pentecostal-Charismatic Movement" (Ph.D. diss., Trinity Evangelical Divinity School, 2011), 223-57.

26. Bill Jackson, "A Short History of the Association of Vineyard Churches," in *Church, Identity, and Change: Theology and Denominational Structures in Unsettled Times,* ed. David A. Roozen and James R. Nieman (Grand Rapids: Eerdmans, 2005), 134.

27. Lonnie Frisbee was one of the more significant figures coming out of the Jesus People. Prior to his involvement in Wimber's congregation, he had been instrumental in the dramatic events that had occurred at the Calvary Chapel in Costa Mesa, California. He had ministered in that church as well as enabling it to create a bridge to the hippie or youth subculture. See David Di Sabatino, *Frisbee: The Life and Death of a Hippie Preacher,* DVD (Garden Grove, CA: Jester Media, 2006).

28. Jackson, "A Short History of the Association of Vineyard Churches," 134-35.

"Power evangelism" became an important emphasis through the 1980s. Thus, in retrospect, May 1980 marked the move of the congregation to more overt, dramatic charismatic manifestations.

## What potential dangers emerged?

As the congregation's way of worship developed, a few potential dangers emerged. One danger was to keep the focus on the centrality of Christ in worship rather than the range of emotional responses. Because God was moving powerfully, bringing his refreshing presence during worship, people needed to be reminded that worship was not about seeking an experience but that it was about seeking Christ: "Worship is not about personality, temperament, personal limitations or church background—it's about God."[29] In Wimber's opinion, God may or may not give an individual a deep spiritual or emotional experience during a service. Thus, he used to correct the way people evaluated a worship service. When he heard people saying "the worship was great" or "the worship was just OK tonight," he gave a different perspective: the whole point of worship was to bless God, so it did not matter how the individual felt. If someone gave his or her heart to God, that should be seen as "good worship."[30]

Another potential hazard was that some expected the worship team to put on a dazzling performance for passive spectators. Wimber worked hard against this notion, surely realizing the possibility for this tendency from his own musical background. John Wimber was very sensitive to using the human power of musical performance and emotional manipulation to produce a response. But he recognized the difference between human effort and the sovereign in-breaking of God's Spirit during worship. Only the presence of the Holy Spirit can transform, renew, and reveal God to the depths of a worshiper's being. The team was to assist the whole congregation to be caught up in the worship of God. Similarly, worship was not to be led by high-powered coercion or manipulation, but by example and invitation. As the leaders drew near to God, the people would follow. Wimber used the example of intimacy between a husband and wife. "You can't force intimacy," he would say.[31]

---

29. Wimber, "The Life-Changing Power," 6.

30. As Sarah Koenig has stated, "The purpose of the Praise and Worship time is simply to worship, which, in the charismatic evangelical sense, means relating with God in an intimate way." Koenig suggests that those who worship in this way sometimes expand the expectations for sacrament to the musical part of a service. Sarah Koenig, "This Is My Daily Bread: Toward a Sacramental Theology of Evangelical Praise and Worship," *Worship* 82, no. 2 (March 2008): 144.

31. Wimber's pastoral concern was very perceptive and is supported by recent research on the emotional power of music. Consider the following statement by Daniel J. Levitin in *This Is Your Brain on Music: The Science of a Human Obsession* (New York: Plume, 2006), 191: "Music appears to mimic some of the features of language and to convey some of the same emotions that vocal communication does, but in a nonreferential and nonspecific way. It also invokes some of the same neural regions that language does, but far more than language, music taps into primitive brain structures involved with motivation, reward, and emotion."

The character of the worship leaders was extremely important. Wimber was concerned about the quality of their discipleship and family life. He made sure he knew the names and family situations of musicians. His relationships with them were real, not merely formal. "Are you still married to the same person?" was his recurring question to insure that they were rightly attentive to family matters. Character building was a frequent topic of John's messages in conferences and to his own congregation in Anaheim. He frequently told a story about visiting a construction site and seeing a hole in the ground that went down several stories. When he asked one of the construction workers why the hole had to be so deep, the workers replied, "You can't build a high tower unless the foundation goes just as deep."

Being Christian was neither simply a business nor a show. Being Christian, rather, was a life—as Williams highlights:

> [Wimber] talked openly, warmly, passionately about his love for Jesus and expressed this in intimate worship. He lived in the Bible so that he could live like the Bible. He experienced the presence and power and gifts of the Spirit operating in his life. He called the gifts tools for ministry that the Spirit would provide on the job as needed. He referenced again and again an intimacy with God where he heard his voice, received revelation in visions, dreams, impressions, prophetic words, and biblical passages.
>
> Wimber had a conversational or dialogical relationship with God. He often prayed with his eyes open. Out of the calling on his own life and his track record of ministry, he enjoyed tremendous spiritual authority. Wimber described himself as "a fat man trying to get to heaven." This was his way of expressing the reality of the supernatural world in which he lived much of the time, especially in quiet devotion or hands-on ministry. His life was pointed beyond this world.[32]

## What is meant by the Kingdom of God?

Understanding Anaheim Vineyard worship is impossible without knowing the overall context of the theological underpinnings and lifestyle of worship that gave rise to its worship songs and services. In terms of key foundations, a theology of the Kingdom of God as the in-breaking of God's rule and reign in present lives had a huge bearing on the week-to-week experience of worship in the early Vineyard. This view was seen not only in welcoming the presence of God through worship music, but also through welcoming his healing, delivering, and saving power. God's presence and power are connected realities. When groups from Vineyard

*Not surprisingly, praying to God in song was important to this congregation. For example, over three-quarters of the songs on an in-house set of 1981 cassette tapes (recorded by Carl Tuttle and Cindy Rethmeier) were prayers. Where else in this volume do you find evidence of this emphasis?*

*Some would critique Wimber's frequent use of the term "supernatural" for creating a sense that God cannot also work through the "natural."*

32. Don Williams, "Theological Perspective and Reflection on the Vineyard Christian Fellowship," in *Church, Identity, and Change: Theology and Denominational Structures in Unsettled Times,* ed. David A. Roozen and James R. Nieman (Grand Rapids: Eerdmans, 2005), 178.

went around the world conducting healing conferences, they always brought a worship team (musicians). The presence of God welcomed in by worship music went hand-in-hand with the presence of God for healing, conviction of sin, and all the gifts of the Holy Spirit, such as prophecy, tongues, and **interpretation**.

Wimber would be attentive during worship to how the Spirit might be moving on that occasion. He sometimes spent the whole worship time looking out over the congregation as he played the keyboard. Then he would speak what God had shown him about worshipers in the congregation. He didn't usually point certain people out to give the word directly to them; instead, he would tell what he "saw in his mind's eye." He called this kind of revelation "**word of knowledge**." Worshipers understood that as they worshiped, the presence of God came, and gifts were released. They didn't worship so that gifts would be released. Rather, the gifts were the overflow of time spent before God, worshiping him.

In describing the work of the Holy Spirit during a worship service, John Wimber pointed out the difference between the permanent indwelling of the Holy Spirit and being "filled with the Spirit" or the "coming upon" of the Holy Spirit. The primary source for this distinction was the book of Acts, in which one sees several occasions of the Holy Spirit filling or "coming upon" the speaker or those listening to a message. (See, for example, Acts 7:55, 8:15–17, 9:17, 10:44–46, 11:15, and 13:9.) While every believer is filled with the Holy Spirit, the "coming upon" of the Holy Spirit can be an often-repeated experience throughout the life of a believer. Thousands of people experienced being filled with the Holy Spirit during worship in the early years of the Anaheim Vineyard. Sometimes there were visible effects of such a visitation of the Holy Spirit but more often the most obvious earmarks were a deep sense of connection with God and an experience of his peace and love. Cindy Rethmeier recalls an example of the Holy Spirit's movement during worship:

> I remember one time in particular in the gymnasium. Worship had just ended, and a man who was sitting in a chair at the end of a row was suddenly in the air, his body flipping backward— from a *sitting* position! John calmly looked over at him and told us it was just the Holy Spirit moving on him, and not to worry about it. I was amazed because no one was praying for him at the time! It happened purely as a result of God's presence on him as we worshiped. Manifestations of power on people's bodies was a fairly common occurrence, but this was a radical example!

John Wimber stressed that the experience of the Kingdom of God within worship should impact how worshipers related to one another and to the world. Wimber believed that the heart of God could be imparted to the church for the poor and the lost as the church waited before him in worship. Indeed, Wimber modeled this for the Anaheim Vineyard as Don Williams points out:

Interpretation is one of the supernatural gifts of the Holy Spirit by which a message delivered in tongues is interpreted by another worshiper for the understanding of the congregation.

Those experiencing the Spirit's movement in demonstrative ways were sometimes ministered to in a separate room, as Wimber describes: "At times, people are quietly led from the larger meeting into our prayer room because they are experiencing a manifestation of God's power such as shaking or weeping." Source: John Wimber, "Zip to 3,000 in 5 Years," *Christian Life* 44, no. 6 (October 1982): 23.

Compassion drove Wimber's commitment to Jesus' healing ministry. He personally prayed for thousands of sick and demonized. He also spearheaded one of the largest relief ministries in Southern California. He insisted that kingdom ministry must be directed to the poor and dispossessed. He wanted to love the church Jesus loved and expended himself to renew it. In a simple sense, from his heart, Wimber wanted to be like Jesus in every area of his life.[33]

### What core values impacted worship services?

Within this broad emphasis on the in-breaking of the Kingdom of God, five core values directly impacted the way worship services were conducted in the early Vineyard. These values drove the fledgling Vineyard congregation and, later, the Vineyard movement. Through his teaching, Wimber instilled these into the Vineyard Fellowship so that they made up its "genetic code."[34]

The first value is Word-driven. The Bible is the absolute authority, the standard and test for life. All supernatural events, prophetic words, and ministry activities were measured by the Scriptures. In frustration, when a parishioner feared manifestations of the Spirit and asked, "How far is this going to go?" Wimber held up a Bible and replied, "No farther than this." He joked later that his response was not as safe as the man thought. Wimber interpreted the Bible from the vantage point of historical exegesis and evangelical faith. He avoided the excesses of allegory and, at the same time, he heard God speaking again and again through his devotional use of Scripture.

Anaheim Vineyard was also Spirit-driven. Wimber viewed the mainline churches as "pneumatically deficient" in contrast to early Christians who were obviously "Spirit people." The drive of the Spirit led to intimacy with God, one of Vineyard's classic worship emphases and what might be said to be the heart theme of Wimber's life. The road to intimacy led through worship, obedience, and surrender to the Spirit. As the Vineyard came into being, Wimber's experiences of the Spirit increased. Power was unleashed as he prayed for people; they were often healed in his living room. Ministry became dynamic and, at times, unpredictable through the presence of the Spirit. One night at the Anaheim Vineyard, the Spirit leveled hundreds of young adults, shaking them and gifting them. Wimber came to see that if Jesus ministered in the Spirit's power, he was foolish to think that he could do without it.

The Anaheim Vineyard was prophetically driven. Although some Quaker elders had theologically suppressed an early experience of "speaking in tongues" in his pre-Vineyard years,

There was some discomfort with the Vineyard movement as seen, for example, in the 1985 review by the conservative Christian Research Institute. Noting Vineyard's doctrinal soundness, the Institute yet wondered if there was enough Bible teaching, if doctrine was de-emphasized, and if personal experience played too large a role. Based on the materials from this congregation, do you think such suspicions were fair or accurate? Source: Elliot Miller et al., "The Vineyard," Christian Research Institute, February 1985, Box 21, John Wimber Collection, Regent University Library Archives, Virginia Beach, Virginia.

---

33. Williams, "Historical-Theological Perspective and Reflection on John Wimber and the Vineyard."

34. The following section is deeply indebted to the insights of Don Williams in his essay cited above: "Historical-Theological Perspective and Reflection on John Wimber and the Vineyard." Much of what follows comes directly from this essay.

Wimber had an intuitive sense of what God was doing and went with it. Once, when a woman prophet wept before him for a half hour, a frustrated Wimber asked her finally to deliver her message. She replied, "That's it" (the weeping). In her tears, he saw the tears of Jesus over him. The episode launched Wimber into doing the "signs and wonders" ministry of Jesus rather than simply preaching Jesus in a strictly evangelical way.[35]

Being prophetically driven meant Wimber led the Vineyard by hearing directly from God. This was not pure subjectivism. He wanted all he heard to be consistent with Scripture and tested by Scripture. Wimber would change course in a sermon because, in the moment, "God told me to." He would wait for direction from the Spirit as he entered into a personal **ministry time** of praying for the sick. He operated in remarkable "words of knowledge," having the ability to identify people God was dealing with in a meeting and knowing surprising details about their lives and needs. He also heard from God in the crisis of making ecclesiastical decisions, often to the dismay of others.[36]

Wimber was pragmatically driven. Through his relationship with Fuller Theological Seminary and its professors' emphasis upon Church Growth principles, Wimber became quite familiar with this approach as an effective way of evangelizing and enlarging churches. He applied the principles directly to the Vineyard. For instance, he applauded and used Calvary Chapel's approach to being "culturally current" in Southern California through informal dress and contemporary music. Similarly, Wimber's services adopted a modified "rock concert" style with an extended set of songs to begin. This set was not mere entertainment, however. It was not to warm up the crowd; it was not an end in itself. Worship was for giving God the praise he deserved and moving the worshiper into an experience of intimacy with him. The congregation became the choir, led by a band up front.[37]

Wimber acknowledged his pragmatic orientation in early descriptions of the congregation. In a 1982 interview, for instance, Wimber described the congregation as a "contemporary church," noting "Because we are young, we are current. We speak the language of these people. Our sermon and songs are familiar and acceptable. We find ourselves communicating eternal truths in a contemporary style." Wimber saw the need to adapt as compelling since "cultural differences have made it difficult for others to relate to the traditional church."[38]

Finally, John Wimber might be said to be spiritually driven. Obvious in his manner was a warm, infectious love for the Son of God, Jesus, most keenly expressed in times of intimate worship. In intimate communion with God, he heard God's voice, received revelation in visions, dreams, impressions, prophetic words, and biblical passages. Wimber—and the

Although Wimber uses the terms "contemporary" and "traditional," they have not yet hardened into the technical terms of the worship wars of the 1990s, when there was widespread use of the term "contemporary worship." Do you remember the first time you heard the term? When and where?

35. Williams, "Theological Perspective and Reflection on the Vineyard Christian Fellowship," 169-71.
36. Williams, "Theological Perspective and Reflection on the Vineyard Christian Fellowship," 171.
37. Williams, "Theological Perspective and Reflection on the Vineyard Christian Fellowship," 175.
38. Wimber, "Zip to 3,000 in 5 Years," 22.

Don Williams describes John's openness to the supernatural realm: "Since Wimber was not socialized by the church as a child, he looked at its institutions and practices as an outsider. This gave him a critical edge. Although he served as a Friends (Quaker) pastor, Wimber failed to merge himself into traditional church life. Not being a product of the modern age church, he escaped the trap of rationalism with its non-supernatural bias." Source: Williams, "Historical-Theological Perspective and Reflection on John Wimber and the Vineyard." http://vineyard indonesia.org/index .php?option=com _content&view=article &id=45%3Aborneo& catid=1%3Alatest& showall=1; accessed July 4, 2008, and January 16, 2013.

worship he led—might be said to realize the reality of God's supernatural world in the conversational informality of Southern California. Simultaneously, Wimber's worship was both culturally accessible and radical. Wimber's radicalism was expressed in his classic statement and question: "I'm a fool for Christ. Whose fool are you?"[39]

## What has been the impact of Vineyard worship?

Thousands of people experienced personal revival as a result of participating in the worship at the Anaheim Vineyard in Southern California in the 1970s, 1980s, and 1990s. The music and focus on the Spirit were some of the primary distinguishing characteristics of this renewal movement that began in Anaheim and spread around the world into more than 50 countries in 20 years. The impact of the Vineyard's worship can be seen in many churches today, sometimes by direct influence and sometimes indirectly. The Vineyard's contribution has come through church planting, publishing, training, conferences, the traveling ministry of Wimber and other Vineyard leaders, as well as simply having worshipers sharing their renewed experiences of God in worship elsewhere. As worshipers sing simple worship songs and God grips their hearts, enabling them to know him intimately, one can see a reflection of the spreading influence of the Anaheim congregation and its pastor, John Wimber.

39. Williams, "Theological Perspective and Reflection on the Vineyard Christian Fellowship," 178.

# Documenting the Community's Worship

## PEOPLE AND ARTIFACTS

The Anaheim Vineyard Congregation in the Early 1980s

The Anaheim Vineyard congregation worshiped in the Canyon High School gymnasium, which it occupied from June 1979 through September 1983. It is difficult to know exactly what was taking place in the service in the picture below, but it appears to be early in the music set. All eyes are up since there are no hand-held texts to draw the face downward. The worshipers did not rely upon projection either. The age of an average worshiper seems quite young.

Source: Bill and Nancy Pfeifer. Used with permission.

The Anaheim Vineyard Congregation Worshiping

The congregation, many with hands raised, has entered into a time of worship. This photograph is another shot in the Canyon High School gymnasium. The worshipers closest to the camera are sitting in the bleachers. The musicians are in the upper left hand corner in front of the yellow curtain. This space is the one in which the revival broke out on Mother's Day, 1980, although the photo is probably not of that occasion.

Source: Bill and Nancy Pfeifer. Used with permission.

The Worship Team

In this photo, Carl Tuttle, on acoustic guitar, leads the worship team. Other musicians visible here and in some of the other photographs include John Wimber (keyboard), Eddie Espinosa (electric guitar), Dick Heying (drums), Mark Curtis (saxophone), and Jerry Davis (bass).

Source: Bill and Nancy Pfeifer. Used with permission.

Dick Heying and his wife, Lynn, were the ones who had invited the Wimbers to the Bible study at which they were converted.

John Wimber Addresses
the Congregation
In casual dress with no
pretentiousness, Wimber
addresses the congrega-
tion. In many ways, the
microphone and keyboard
represent two vital aspects
of Wimber's ministry with
this assembly.

Source: John Wimber, "Zip to
3,000 in 5 Years," *Christian Life*
44, no. 6 (October 1982): 19.
Used with permission.

Prayer Ministry among Vineyard Worshipers

Vineyard worshipers engage in a ministry of prayer to each other as several groups gather around those in need of prayer. John Wimber waits at the keyboard.

Source: John Wimber, "Zip to 3,000 in 5 Years," *Christian Life* 44, no. 6 (October 1982): 21. Used with permission.

The Worship Team Leading Worship

The original caption for this photo when published in 1982 was a kind of Vineyard testimony: "God began taking us—a worn-out bunch of Pharisees—and turning us into a band of followers who no longer are governed by our fears of fanaticism or what people will say about us."

Source: John Wimber, "Zip to 3,000 in 5 Years," *Christian Life* 44, no. 6 (October 1982): 22. Used with permission.

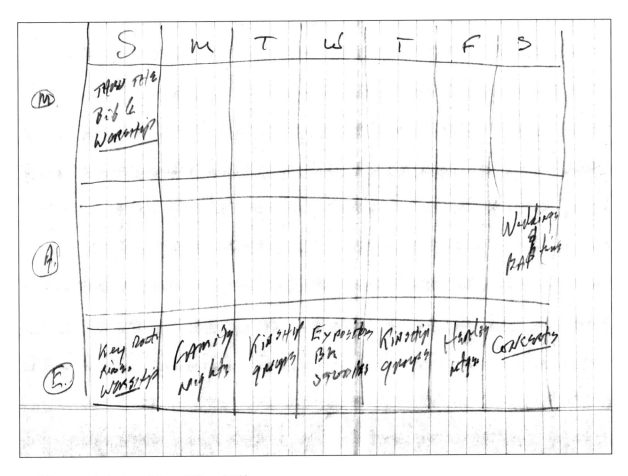

Weekly Schedule for Worship and Church Life

Despite being a new congregation, the Anaheim Vineyard's weekly schedule was a busy one. Congregational worship occurred on Sunday morning and evening. Other occasions for worship happened in the smaller Kinship groups and on other occasions. A sense of this rhythm can be found in this handwritten schema, presumably in Wimber's handwriting, located with other planning documents in a folder entitled "Plans for '78." Note the reference to healing meetings on Friday nights, weddings and baptisms on Saturday afternoons, and concerts on Saturday nights.

Source: Box 16, John Wimber Collection, Regent University Library Archives, Virginia Beach, Virginia. Used with permission.

*Songs of the Vineyard*
Cover and Advertisement

This image of worshipers from the Old Testament was a popular one in the early Vineyard movement for publication of song collections and educational conference materials. As shown below, the first volume of *Songs of the Vineyard* used Gustave Doré's "Jephthah's Daughter Coming to Meet Her Father," based on Judges 11:34, as its cover.[1] Notice the expressive use of the body and the multiple musical instruments. In these respects, this representation of biblical worship is intended as an image for Vineyard worship. The advertisement of the songbook in the May 1985 issue of *First Fruits*, the fledgling denomination's magazine, is also included below.

Source: The image of the cover is from the original. The advertisement is from the May 1985 issue of *First Fruits* (p. 19) as found in Box 2 in the John Wimber Collection, Regent University Library Archives, Virginia Beach, Virginia. Used with permission.

1. We are indebted to Mark Torgerson for identifying the illustration.

| | SUNDAY | MONDAY | TUESDAY | WEDNESDAY | THURSDAY | FRIDAY | SATURDAY |
|---|---|---|---|---|---|---|---|
| | 4 | 5 | 6 | 7 | 8 | 9 | 10 |
| morning | | | | Lonnie Frisbee w/ John Bond October 7 - 11 | Frisbee: Bond / Professional team arrives Johannesburg | Frisbee: Bond | Wimber: Dutch Reform / Frisbee: Bond / Thompson: Hatfield / Stipe: Other churches |
| afternoon | | | Lonnie Frisbee arrives Johannesburg | FREE | FREE | FREE | FREE |
| evening | | Professional Team leaves Los Angles | Frisbee: Bond. | | Frisbee: Bond / Other professional team members free | Lay team leaves Los Angeles / Frisbee: Bond / Wimber: Dutch Reform / Thompson: Hatfield Baptist / Stipe: Other churches | Frisbee: Bond / Thompson: Hatfield / Wimber: Dutch Reform / Stipe: Other churches |
| | 11 | 12 | 13 | 14 | 15 | 16 | 17 |
| morning | Frisbee: Bond / Wimber: Dutch Reform / Thompson: Hatfield Baptist / Stipe: Other churches | DAY OFF | FREE | Pastor's conference 9:00 a.m. - 1:00 p.m. Wimber | Pastor's conference 9:00 a.m. - 1:00 p.m. Wimber | Pastor's conference 9:00 a.m. - 1:00 p.m. Wimber | Worship seminar 9:00 a.m. - 2:00 p.m. Tuttle |
| afternoon | FREE | DAY OFF | Lay Team arrives from Los Angeles | FREE | FREE | FREE | FREE |
| evening | Frisbee: Bond / Wimber: Dutch Reform / Thompson: Hatfield Baptist / Stipe: Other churches | DAY OFF | Host and housing assignment | City wide rally-Johannesburg | City wide rally Johannesburg | City wide rally Johannesburg | City wide rally Johannesburg |
| | 18 | 19 | 20 | 21 | 22 | 23 | 24 |
| morning | Pastors and six ministry teams | DAY OFF | Travel to Capetown | Pastor's conference 9:00 a.m. - 1:00 p.m. Wimber | Pastor's conference 9:00 a.m. - 1:00 p.m. Wimber | Pastor's conference 9:00 a.m. - 1:00 p.m. Wimber | Wimber, Korea Team leaves for Seoul / Worship seminar - Tuttle 9:00 a.m. - 2:00 p.m. |
| afternoon | In Johannesburg churches all day | DAY OFF | FREE | FREE | FREE | FREE | FREE |
| evening | 1. Wimber 2. Thompson 3. Tuttle 4. Frisbee 5. Stipe | DAY OFF | Host and housing assignments | City wide rally-Capetown | City wide rally Capetown | City wide rally Capetown | City wide rally Capetown |
| | 25 | 26 | 27 | 28 | | | |
| morning | Pastors and four ministry teams | Teams leave for Los Angeles | | | | | |
| afternoon | In Capetown churches all day | | | | | | |
| evening | 1. Thompson 2. Tuttle 3. Stipe 4. Frisbee | | | | | | |

TENTATIVE SCHEDULE: SOUTH AFRICA MINISTRY TOUR OCTOBER 5-26, 1981

CALENDAR

Schedule for the 1981 Trip to South Africa

By the early 1980s, ministry teams from the Anaheim Vineyard congregation were traveling overseas. In addition to preaching and conducting times of prayer ministry for healing, deliverance, and other miracles, time was given to teaching on worship. In this way, the approach to worship that had developed in Anaheim spread around the world. The following schedule from an October 1981 trip to South Africa shows that the better part of two Saturdays, one in Johannesburg and one in Cape Town, were devoted to a worship seminar taught by Carl Tuttle. The engagement letter from Wimber to Tuttle instructed the latter to bring overheads, teaching notes, and 300–400 cassette tapes to sell.

Source: Found in *First Fruits* (June 1984): 14. Located in Box 2, John Wimber Collection, Regent University Library Archives, Virginia Beach, Virginia. Used with permission.

1982 Trip to England

In addition to traveling to South Africa, ministry teams from Anaheim Vineyard made trips to England early in the congregation's existence. The worship and ministry which occurred in California spread quickly on these trips. Such trips, including John Wimber's ministry, made a large impact upon the charismatic community in England, especially within the Church of Eng-

land. These images show activities during the church's second trip to England in 1982. The first photograph is of the renowned Jesus People evangelist Lonnie Frisbee preaching. The other photographs show prayers being offered and received by participants. Prayer during the ministry times was widespread, and it was never just the work of clergy.

Matt Redman, the well-known British worship leader and songwriter, experienced worship with a Vineyard team on one of their trips to England. He tells of the impact that experience had on him: "I was seven years old when I first came across the Vineyard values in worship. John Wimber and a big team showed up in Chorleywood, England, where I lived, and my Mum took me along to a couple of the meetings." The experience still influences Redman: "More than anything I was struck by how 'real' it all seemed. There was a strong sense of 'encounter'—the people of God, in the presence of God, pouring out the praises of God. . . . Looking back those couple of meetings had a profound effect on me—and still now affect how I worship Jesus."[2] Like it did Redman, the Vineyard has and continues to influence Christian worship worldwide.

Source: Cindy Rethmeier. Used with permission.

2. John Wimber, *The Way In Is the Way On* (Atlanta: Ampelon Publishing, 2006), 105.

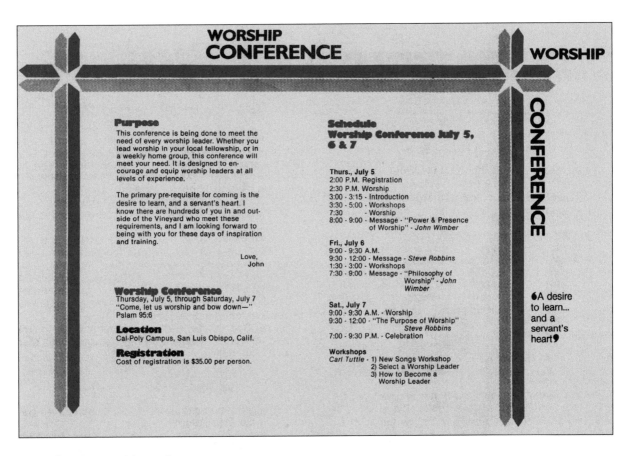

**WORSHIP CONFERENCE**

**WORSHIP CONFERENCE**

**Purpose**

This conference is being done to meet the need of every worship leader. Whether you lead worship in your local fellowship, or in a weekly home group, this conference will meet your need. It is designed to encourage and equip worship leaders at all levels of experience.

The primary pre-requisite for coming is the desire to learn, and a servant's heart. I know there are hundreds of you in and outside of the Vineyard who meet these requirements, and I am looking forward to being with you for these days of inspiration and training.

Love,
John

**Worship Conference**
Thursday, July 5, through Saturday, July 7
"Come, let us worship and bow down—"
Pslam 95:6

**Location**
Cal-Poly Campus, San Luis Obispo, Calif.

**Registration**
Cost of registration is $35.00 per person.

**Schedule**
**Worship Conference July 5, 6 & 7**

**Thurs., July 5**
2:00 P.M. Registration
2:30 P.M. Worship
3:00 - 3:15 · Introduction
3:30 - 5:00 · Workshops
7:30         · Worship
8:00 - 9:00 · Message · "Power & Presence of Worship" · *John Wimber*

**Fri., July 6**
9:00 - 9:30 A.M.
9:30 - 12:00 - Message · *Steve Robbins*
1:30 - 3:00 - Workshops
7:30 - 9:00 - Message · "Philosophy of Worship" · *John Wimber*

**Sat., July 7**
9:00 - 9:30 A.M. · Worship
9:30 - 12:00 - "The Purpose of Worship" *Steve Robbins*
7:00 - 9:30 P.M. · Celebration

**Workshops**
*Carl Tuttle* · 1) New Songs Workshop
2) Select a Worship Leader
3) How to Become a Worship Leader

*A desire to learn... and a servant's heart*

Notice for 1984 Worship Conference

The following announcement for a 1984 training conference, printed in the denominational magazine, is an example of the effort to train worship leaders, i.e., musicians who lead worship, for congregational and Kinship group settings. In the 1980s, corporate and small group worship settings using guitars grew quickly not only in the Anaheim congregation but in other churches as well. Note the combination of speakers and topics addressed.

Source: Found in *First Fruits* (June 1984): 14. Located in Box 2, John Wimber Collection, Regent University Library Archives, Virginia Beach, Virginia. Used with permission.

## Worship Setting and Space

Freedom of Expression

This picture is from the floor level of a service in the Canyon High School gymnasium. As the music team leads the singing, worshipers show a variety of responses. Some sit. Others sit with hands raised. Some stand with hands raised. They offer their worship and hearts to God. Notice in this picture it seems the men in the congregation are the first to stand.

Source: Bill and Nancy Pfeifer. Used with permission.

A Sea of Worshipers

Almost all the congregation is engaged in outward expressions of love. Standing, hands raised, and singing their love for God, the congregation overwhelms the musicians visually in this photo. Canyon High School's school song and a painting of its mascot (a Comanche) fill the side wall.

Source: Bill and Nancy Pfeifer. Used with permission.

The Musicians' Platform from the Side

This photograph shows the proximity of the congregation to the musicians in the school gymnasium. Congregational seating extended up to the slightly raised platform. Although only men are on the platform in this picture, Cindy Rethmeier would join them when a female vocalist was needed in a song. John Wimber supported and encouraged women as worship leaders.

Source: Bill and Nancy Pfeifer. Used with permission.

Later Arrangement of Space

Whereas the early arrangements in the gymnasiums had the music team closer to the people, later arrangements used a layout that has since become widespread. In this later photograph of Anaheim Vineyard worship from the mid-1980s, the musicians occupy a stage at the front of the congregation.

Source: Tim Stafford, "Testing the Wine from John Wimber's Vineyard" *Christianity Today* 30, no. 11 (August 8, 1986): 21. Used with permission.

# Descriptions of Worship

*Worship in a Home: Origins of the Anaheim Vineyard Congregation*

*From time to time, John and Carol Wimber reminisced about the origins of Vineyard. In the following excerpt, taken from a booklet that John handed out to members of his congregation in 1982, he chronicles the journey on which God had taken the church. In the foreword, John notes the therapeutic nature of the worship and the community.[1]*

Shifting how worshipers related to God—from duty to gift—was critical. The songs they sang expressed the wonder and vitality of God's graciousness. In Christian history, such shifts have often been the trigger for major movements. In the 18th century, for example, John Wesley was propelled into dynamic ministry by moving from the "faith of a servant" to the "faith of a child." With such a shift, it is no longer a matter of what one can earn as a reward from a demanding God but what one receives as a gift from a loving God.

In late 1976, a small group of believers began to meet together in a home to seek the Lord. None of us realized our true state of spiritual ill-health. We knew we were weak and tired. But we had no idea how weak. Some of those who gathered together had been trying for years to serve the Lord. Others were excited in their new faith but not really going anywhere. God in His mercy opened our eyes. We saw ourselves. It was a painful experience. The church that became the Vineyard Christian Fellowship was born on Mother's Day, 1977.

When we gathered together, all we could do was sing to the Lord. As we worshiped, we began to get well. We began to feel a spiritual strength come into our lives—strength we had never known before. Worship had opened the door to a relationship with God that was totally new for us. We no longer felt compelled to "do things for God." We began to enjoy Him and our relationship with Him. . . .

Our relationship with God affected our relationship to each other. No longer did we feel the urgent need to press others into a mold. People were free to be themselves and develop in their faith at their own pace. We were pulled forward by the ever-growing health of the body as it began to gain strength and spiritual intensity. Relationship with God, each other and with the world have been forever altered for those who have been involved in our fellowship.

1. Unpublished, undated manuscript, distributed within the congregation. Used with permission.

Essentially what the Lord has done over the last five years is to create a healing environment. People get help just by being here. We often refer to ourselves as "The Church of the Walking Wounded." That is what we were and still are.

*In a 1983 sermon John Wimber reflects on his initial experience of the home-based worship, especially his own puzzlement and discomfort.*[2]

A few years ago when God began speaking to us as a group, it was really just a small group, maybe six or seven people, they were meeting in a home in the other side of the Canyon and God began speaking to them about worship. They would just gather together and sing, sometimes two or three hours at a time. By the time I first attended, the group had already grown to fifty or sixty, and the worship was really very intense. I remember sitting there the first time and thought, "What are they doing?" because they would sing one song after another. The people would, without any structure or order, would kneel, some of them would lay down on the floor, some of them would stand-up and lean against the wall, others would be sitting on chairs. And it really bothered me that nobody was taking control of this thing and organizing it. I remember going home to my wife, and I said, "Nothing is ever going to come of that. They don't have any leaders. There is no one telling them what to do." She looked at me and gasped and said, "What about the Lord?" And I said, "Well, what about Him?" [And she answered,] "He is telling people what to do." I said, "Really?" She said, "Yes." I said, "That's far out. Right here in Yorba Linda. How can that be?"

Over the next few months God began teaching me how to worship. And I have shared with you before that it was very difficult for me, and I am not sure that it's all that easy for everybody, for many of us it is maybe more difficult than others because we are not really very in tune with any kind of a public demonstration, or maybe very assertive or very open to displaying emotions, or getting involved in any kind of a public way. I would much rather be a spectator at an event than being a participator. So it is my inclination to go and watch and sit back, rather than get involved.

. . . when I first started coming to the group and they began worshiping, I was really intimidated by some people. You know some people just get into it. You know what I mean. It is like they didn't have a bone in their body. Their hands would be up in the air. They would be on the floor. They would be crying. They would be kneeling. They would be sitting. They would be laying prostrate with their face down. It really "bugged" me. I didn't like it. I wished they would control themselves. I thought they were too emotional. And then one night the Lord touched me and I forgot all about that. I found myself doing some of the same things. At

Imagine that you were a first-time visitor uncomfortable with Vineyard's worship. What effect would Wimber's description of his own discomfort have on you?

2. From a presentation entitled "Worship" in "Basic Priorities of Vineyard Christian Fellowship," Box 13, John Wimber Collection, Regent University Library Archives, Virginia Beach, Virginia, 1-2, 10-11.

first I thought it was a personality trait. And if so, it's catching. Obedience to God requires the discipline of worship. God has called us to worship Him.

*Carol Wimber speaks of redefining the term "worship" in the early history of the congregation. The new way of thinking of "worship" put the emphasis on speaking directly and lovingly to the Lord, especially in song.*[3]

We began worship with nothing but a sense of calling from the Lord to a deeper relationship with him. Before we started meeting in a small home church setting in 1977,[4] the Holy Spirit had been working in my heart, creating a tremendous hunger for God.

One day as I was praying, the word "worship" appeared in my mind like a newspaper headline. I had never thought much about that word before. As an evangelical Christian I had always assumed the entire Sunday morning gathering was "worship"—and, in a sense, I was correct. But in a different sense there were particular elements of the service that were especially devoted to worship and not to teaching, announcements, musical presentations, and all the other activities that are part of a typical Sunday morning gathering. I had to admit that I wasn't sure which part of the service was supposed to be worship.

After we started to meet in our home gathering, I noticed times during the meeting—usually when we sang—in which I experienced God deeply. We sang many songs, but mostly songs about worship or testimonies from one Christian to another. But occasionally we sang a song personally and intimately to Jesus, with lyrics like "Jesus, I love you."[5] Those types of songs both stirred and fed the hunger for God within me.

About this time I began asking our music leader[6] why some songs seemed to spark something in us and others didn't. As we talked about worship, we realized that often we would sing about worship yet we never actually worshiped—except when we accidentally stumbled onto intimate songs like "I Love You, Lord," and "I Lift My Voice."[7] Thus, we began to see a difference between songs about Jesus and songs to Jesus.

Now, during this time when we were stumbling around corporately in worship, many of us were also worshiping at home alone. During these solitary times we were not necessarily singing, but we were bowing down, kneeling, lifting hands, and praying spontaneously in the Spirit—sometimes with spoken prayers, sometimes with non-verbalized prayers, and even prayers without words at all. We noticed that as our individual worship life deepened, when

"Worship" was being redefined in a way that connected it most closely to the time of extended singing, which included experiencing God.

Again, note how critical the distinction between singing to and singing about is. Can the distinction be overemphasized? Perhaps. Looking at biblical prayers and songs addressed to God in worship, one can see that often biblical worshipers spoke to God in ways that often spoke about God in great detail and length. Remembering God's activity is a biblical and classic way of speaking to God.

3. Carol Wimber's reminiscing is found in John Wimber, "Worship: Intimacy with God," in *Thoughts on Worship* (Anaheim, CA: Vineyard Music Group, 1996), 1-3.

4. This date is likely a misprint since other accounts place the origins in 1976.

5. The precise song in question cannot be identified.

6. This surely refers to Carl Tuttle.

7. The reference to "I Love You, Lord" is likely the song written by Laurie Klein, copyrighted in 1978, 1980 by House of Mercy Music. The song "I Lift My Voice" cannot be identified with certainty. The reference may be to a line in the Laurie Klein song.

we came together, there was a greater hunger toward God. So we learned that what happens when we are alone with the Lord determines how intimate and deep the worship will be when we come together.

About that time we realized our worship blessed God, that it was for God alone and not just a vehicle of preparation for the pastor's sermon. This was an exciting revelation. After learning about the central place of worship in our meetings, there were many instances in which all we did was worship God for an hour or two.

At this time we also discovered that singing was not the only way to worship God. Because the word worship means literally to bow down, it is important that our bodies are involved in what our spirits are saying. In scripture this is accomplished through bowing heads, lifting hands, kneeling, and even lying prostrate before God.

A result of our worshiping and blessing God is being blessed by him. We don't worship God in order to get blessed, but we are blessed as we worship him. He visits his people with manifestation of the Holy Spirit.

Thus worship has a two-fold aspect: communication with God through the basic means of singing and praying and communication from God through teaching and preaching the word, prophecy, exhortation, etc. We lift him up and exalt him and as a result are drawn into his presence where he speaks to us.

*Bob Fulton, one of the earliest members of the staff at the Anaheim Vineyard, reflects on his participation in the home meeting in late 1976, this meeting's impact on the congregation's way of worship, and the continued emphasis upon home-based small groups ("Kinship" groups) as a place for fellowship, worship, and ministry. Fulton wrote his reflection as an explanation for the sake of the growing nation-wide Vineyard movement.*[8]

People were coming through the door with mixed expressions. Some were excited, happy, enthusiastic; others were calm and reserved, while still others looked confused and bewildered. They found a place to sit and talk as the crowd gathered.

We had been meeting for eight or nine weeks now and the faces were more than names to me; they were reflections of the work of God. One man, who had become a Christian several years previously but had gone back to his old life style, had a big contagious smile on his face. Just two weeks previously he came to the meeting discouraged and despondent, but as we worshiped and talked about what God was beginning to do to us, he started to cry and confess his sins. He was sharing with a small group of people and as they ministered to him, he became free again. He now comes to seek to know God better along with the rest of us.

A woman, who had a difficult time staying in contact with God, began seeing her life

Whether in the home or in public buildings, the fledgling congregation grew rapidly. In what ways would experiences such as these have attracted new members?

8. Bob Fulton, "The Genesis of Vineyard Kinships," *First Fruits* (February 1985): 6-7.

change. She had tried to read the Bible, pray and go to church, but the temptations of her past were too strong. Tired of giving into her sin and thinking everyone else was doing so well, she had resigned herself to Christian life which was up one day and down the next. Change in her life began to occur as she came and relationships within the group gelled. Others were there to give forgiveness, strength and exhortation to her. God used commitment of those within the group to overpower the strength of her history. As the destructive patterns changed, her walk with God became more intimate and consistent.

This group was the beginning of the Small Group ministry in the Vineyard. At least it was the pattern for what we call Kinship Groups. To understand why we do what we do when we meet, it's beneficial to remember what God did to us. He gave us acceptance, forgiveness, and freedom to come boldly to him with all that is on our hearts.

John [Wimber] came to the group several months after it was formed and helped us to see what was happening to us. His background as a Church Growth consultant was beneficial in analyzing what God was doing. In a small group training setting he reflected back to us what we had been going through.

Phrases like "seek his face," "hunger for God" and "intimacy with the living God" became common with us. The songs that Carl Tuttle brought to us caused a breaking in our inner being. Our spirits began to open to hear God's voice, and we saw how desperate we were. John began to share that the worship which we were experiencing with God was our highest priority. If we had to stop doing all that we were doing, one thing would remain, worship. Worship helped us to develop intimacy with God so we could hear him speak to us and distinguish his voice from all other voices.

One of the most obvious ways to worship was through singing to God. We were empty and did not know it. We were religious, broken and deaf. First person expressions, like "I Love You, Lord,"[9] "You Are My Hiding Place,"[10] and "Change My Heart, O God,"[11] caused a face to face encounter with God. Previously we just sang songs about God, but now our words brought about an intense, intimate expressive worship to God. With our eyes closed and our hands raised, we would fall on our knees without realizing what we were doing. This body language helps our spirits express our thoughts to him.

We had long been exposed to worship which was more entertainment, and this form became more and more distasteful as we learned a new form of worship. The way we controlled our own worship previously had actually suppressed our spirits. It was so comfortable to

*The simplicity and repetitiveness of the lyrics enable the full use of the body in worship. Does having to handle a songbook limit physical expressiveness?*

9. The reference to "I Love You, Lord" is likely the song written by Laurie Klein, copyrighted in 1978, 1980 by House of Mercy Music. Notice that Carol Wimber in her reminiscing identified the same song.

10. This song is likely Michael Ledner's "You Are My Hiding Place," copyrighted in 1981 by CCCM Music/Universal Music—Brentwood Benson Publishing.

11. Perhaps Fulton is referring to a song by Eddie Espinosa, one of the early music leaders in the congregation. The lyrics for "Change My Heart, O God" were copyrighted in 1982 by Mercy/Vineyard Publishing. Fulton is likely projecting this later song into an earlier period as an example of the type of song he had in mind.

sing about life in God, but it could not satisfy the longings of our inner beings. This break-ing process is not comfortable at all, but it is satiable. In the Vineyard we began and desire to continue as a group of people who found a hunger for more of God and a song to cry out to him in worship.

There is a definite atmosphere that worship creates. Worship gave people a sense of safety and openness. People were encouraged to share from a personal point of view, using the word "I" instead of "we." As intimacy with God increased, fellowship with one another become more personal and open. People were able to say where they really were without the fear of rejection.

The way we had formally criticized those who were trapped in a sin or weakness changed. Somehow we were now *for* each other, with a drive to see each other freed from entrapment. Now there was a feeling of protection, as we gathered, that allowed us to talk about our sin so that we were forgiven and released from its power.

Sometimes criticism is aimed at worship services that use more "I" language than "we" language. What does Fulton identify as the beneficial aspects of using very personal language? Do you agree?

## Testimonies from Early Participants

*Many of the people from those early days of the Anaheim Vineyard are still around. Here are some of their memories about its worship. Some of these reminiscences in shortened form were used above.*

*The first is from Todd Hunter, a former Vineyard church planter and assistant to Wimber in the Association of Vineyard Churches. He was a close pastoral associate of Wimber from the early days. He and his wife, Debbie, moved to Wheeling, West Virginia, in 1979, as the first church planters out of the Anaheim Vineyard. Hunter speaks first on the distinctive quality of the congregation's worship.*[12]

For 25 years I've traveled all over the world; I've participated in worship services, conferences, seminars, retreats and just about every other setting in which Christian worship takes place. In my judgment, the worship in the early era of Calvary Chapel/Vineyard Yorba Linda stands out way above the rest—it is of a completely different nature.

Though John Wimber was a professional arranger and performer, and while the remain-der of the band and singers were competent, neither of those qualities are the difference-makers. I've heard better musicians and much better vocalists; I've experienced far more complex and professional arrangements than we were familiar with at church week after week.

Hunter's testimony reflects the fluid nature of the congre-gation's name and location in the early years. The congrega-tion was first associ-ated with Calvary Chapels, another Southern California movement, and was located in Yorba Linda, not Anaheim.

12. Todd Hunter, electronic mail to Cindy Rethmeier, May 20, 2006.

*Todd Hunter says that the three distinguishing characteristics of early Vineyard worship were intimacy with God, the manifest presence of the Holy Spirit, and an expectancy that God would visit his church and act powerfully during every time of worship. Here he describes the congregation's desire for intimacy and its eager anticipation for worshiping together.*[13]

The vast majority of us were sincerely and innocently trying to deal with God; he had initiated a relationship with us and we wanted to know him more. Thus we were open with our worship, praise, adoration, petition, etc. We were gently, but expertly, guided by our pastors into what it meant to be honest and free in worship. Interestingly, in the early days, none of this "freedom" or "honesty" resulted in weird or self-serving behaviors. The whole atmosphere was simple, tender and God-focused. . . .

We literally could not wait to get to church—to be in the congregation, to worship, to see what God would do today, etc. We felt anticipation, and we had legitimate hope that God would visit us in worship because he was consistent in doing so.

For several years, these three elements—intimacy, manifest presence, and expectancy—became not a "vicious cycle" but a "benevolent cycle" that created truly amazing and, in retrospection, rare worship. We hungered for God, he "showed up" as we used to say in our Southern California slang, and this in turn created increased expectancy. This went on and on for years; many people walked into worship services for the first time and were caught up into the cycle and the atmosphere it created without ever giving it a conscious thought, except in hindsight: 'What just happened to me? Why do I feel so loved and so full of love, so close to God, so willing to pour out my heart to God in worship, to serve others, etc?' I don't ever remember anyone walking out of the gym and remarking about the band, the great guitar licks, the cool piano chops or the amazing vocal performances. It was all about feeling and knowing the presence of God and responding to him in worship.

*Mike and Char Turrigiano, senior pastors of the New York City Vineyard Fellowship, speak about their initial experiences in Vineyard worship. Their relationship with the Vineyard movement began in 1980 when they met and were apprenticed by John Wimber. First, Char Turrigiano testifies:*[14]

I would have to say that before I visited the Vineyard church in the High School, I did not really know what real worship was. . . . I came into the gym and sat down and was quite overwhelmed by the natural, down to earth experience that was different from any church I had been to before. When John Wimber sat at the piano and played the first chord, I immediately started crying, and felt a presence that was so overwhelming, I realized this

In the larger history of Christianity, Vineyard worship falls within a larger tradition known as Pietism, which emphasizes a close connection between knowing God and the heart. The emphasis on feeling God's presence in worship has been common for several hundred years.

---

13. Todd Hunter, electronic mail to Cindy Rethmeier, May 20, 2006.
14. Char Turrigiano, electronic mail to Cindy Rethmeier, May 19, 2006.

must be the Holy Spirit (duh), and I experienced an intimacy [with God] that I had not before. I felt like the words were piercing my heart and I realized I was experiencing love, grace, mercy and God himself was there with me. I suddenly realized that worship was an experience between me and God and in this case music was the tool in which he was meeting me. I remember singing "Change my heart, O God"[15] and immediately I wanted to change my heart. So this for me was an experience that changed my life forever!

*Mike Turrigiano, likewise, had a moving experience in his first taste of Vineyard worship.*[16]

My first exposure to what was later to become known as "Vineyard worship" was in Canyon High School gymnasium in Yorba Linda, California, back in 1981. My world was rocked in a church service led by John Wimber. Up until that time I was used to Pentecostal, pep rally brand worship—mostly anthems and choruses about God—not very personal. However on this day, as Carl Tuttle started singing "Isn't He beautiful? /Beautiful, isn't He?",[17] I was gripped by an overwhelming longing for God as the Spirit melted my heart. I started crying. . . .

*Linda Pardee and her husband, Dave, grew up in Southern California and became Christians through the early ministry of John Wimber in 1981. Through the years they have planted two Vineyard congregations on the West Coast and worked on the staff at the original Anaheim Vineyard. Here are Linda Pardee's memories of early Vineyard worship:*[18]

It was relational, intimate and as I observed others lifting their hands, kneeling, crying and singing songs like "O Lord, you're beautiful,"[19] I found this to be *way too intimate and vulnerable to enter into at first.* As I started to sing the words to the song, something seemed to break inside of me and I found myself weeping as if I was this child I was singing about. At that point I felt my hardened heart begin to soften. This God that I thought I knew, who was so distant and uncaring, was drawing me into a place where He could show me a love I had never known before.

Many of these testimonies of early Vineyard worship experience note the unusual quality (at first) of such intensely personal worship. The notions of intimacy and vulnerability are not that common in the long history of Christian worship. How might the culture of Southern California in the 1970s have shaped worshipers to want to experience God in such ways?

15. Turrigiano is referring to "Change My Heart, O God," a song by Eddie Espinosa, one of the early music leaders in the congregation. The lyrics for the song were copyrighted in 1982 by Mercy/Vineyard Publishing.

16. Mike Turrigiano, electronic mail to Cindy Rethmeier, May 20, 2006.

17. The song "Isn't He" was written by John Wimber and copyrighted in 1980 by Mercy/Vineyard Publishing.

18. Linda Pardee, electronic mail to Cindy Rethmeier, May 31, 2006.

19. The song "O Lord, You're Beautiful" was written by Keith Green and copyrighted in 1980 by Capital CMG—Brentwood Benson Publishing.

*Penny Fulton, the sister of Carol Wimber and the wife of Bob Fulton, was a staff member from the very early days of the Anaheim Vineyard. She points out the wooing, drawing, and convicting work of the Holy Spirit in worship.*[20]

My experience of worship began when I was in a home group with my friends that I became Christians with 12 years earlier. This group eventually became the beginning of the Vineyard movement. We had become rather caustic in our Christian experience and met together to somehow understand what had happened to the expectancy we once had.

    . . . At first, I was just embarrassed over the intimacy that was expressed out loud directly to God. Such intimacy made me close my eyes and not look at the others. The words were all about adoring God and laying my life down before Him. I had never sung songs to God before, just about Him. This felt uncomfortable. I remember once wanting to leave because something just felt like 'too much.' I'm so grateful I didn't run away.

    The more I sang those words, the more I realized how far away I'd gone from Him. I think that was the uncomfortable feeling that I wanted to hide from. But facing the truth brought such a feeling of God's love falling on me in waves. There was no way I could hide behind religiosity anymore. The words we were singing were so simple and real, yet pierced through to the very heart of God.

    God was cutting through the tough religious exterior of committed Christians who had been hardened through the battles of life and the rigors of being in church leadership. He was extending a simple grace-filled message. "Come to me, lay your burdens down . . . seek me as your Lord, your portion, your treasure . . . let me love you."

Much of the early Vineyard material shows a parallel emphasis upon the worshiper's heart and God's heart. The worship is "heart to heart" in many respects. God pours out an awareness of divine love into the worshiper's heart, and the (sung) worship pours out adoration that touches the heart of God.

### Early Participants' Recollections about the Music

*Carl Tuttle, the leader of the musical team, describes the simplicity of worship planning and leading in the congregation's early years. This simplicity fits with the congregation's approach to go through the music to become centered on the Lord himself during worship.*[21] *Tuttle's recollections highlight, too, one of the difficulties in writing a full history of this congregation: the lack of a paper trail left from the early years that would document some of the specifics of these early services. In addition, as this remembrance suggests, Tuttle and others were key shapers of this community's worship although some of the first histories of the movement have a hard time broadening the spotlight to include more than John Wimber, the charismatic senior pastor.*

We launched on May 10, 1977. The worship team consisted of John [Wimber], myself, and

20. Penny Fulton, electronic mail to Cindy Rethmeier, May 20, 2006.
21. Carl Tuttle, electronic mail to Andy Park, August 1, 2008.

Dick Heying. John [was] on a Rhodes piano, me on acoustic guitar, I'm sure it was mic'd at the time, and Dick on drums. Jerry Davis joined the team that night as a result of walking by John after the service and John asking if he still played bass.

Our preparation consisted of showing up prior to the service and tuning up to the Rhodes. From that May until May 1983, we never practiced or rehearsed anything; there was never a set list, nor any female singers. I just hit the first chord and away we went and the guys followed. I never wrote out a set list, even for myself. When there was a female part, Cindy [Rethmeier] was handed a mic off stage at floor level. It was because the stage was 8'x16' and there was no room. By this time, Eddie Espinosa[22] was playing lead guitar.

During this period, the emphasis was on consistency and modeling of an approach to worship in terms of team members. From 1977–83, the same team played. I only recall missing 3–4 times and John only missed a handful; he was committed the first 5 years to being there on Sundays as we established ourselves. When John was away, Peter Jacobs from the group "Children of the Day" would fill in and when Dick Heying (on drums) missed a Sunday, Ron Tutt (who had played for Elvis and Neil Diamond) filled in. That was pretty cool.

At that time John didn't want to construct another team, nor rotate people in and out. He and Carol [Wimber] felt—and they were right—that we were establishing a prototype.

We did raise up dozens of worship leaders. I think Cindy and I did one of the first Worship Training tapes ever. At that time the term "worship" hadn't entered the vernacular. We "produced" two cassette tapes, which included me tuning my guitar so people could tune to the tape. Cindy and I went into a bathroom and the "engineer" was out in the living room recording on a reel to reel. We gave this out to those who were learning to lead worship for small groups. . . .

Now this is the absolute truth: during this period, John Wimber, the senior pastor of the church, never even once asked me what we were going to sing! In that period of time, he never directed me what to do or not to do, other than to cut a song or something because of baby dedications or something like that. Again, I think John saw this as a formational period and had the restraint and wisdom not to mess with it too much. Even though it was simple and frankly repetitive—we didn't have the abundance of songs we have today—it was very impactful and people drove for hours to come to our Sunday night service.

I am not suggesting at all that this is the best approach: no monitors, no rehearsal, no clear direction, it was just the way it was during that time and it was good. The restraint John showed was remarkable; he was a trained musician, [and] the senior leader of the church. He certainly could have exerted his authority or interjected himself, but he didn't, [and] it was remarkable, especially since he was sitting right there playing the keys and had a vocal mic.

In what ways could Tuttle's approach be seen as a contemporizing of the classic Quaker dependence upon the Holy Spirit's immediate moving in worship? The simple nature of the songs—remember that the congregation were not given printed lyrics— enabled this approach.

From such simple beginnings, the Vineyard movement has become one of the main influences on Protestant worship in the latter part of the 20th century.

---

22. Espinosa composed the well-known song entitled "Change My Heart, O God."

As far as the songs we sang: Sunday mornings about 30 minutes, Sunday nights 45 minutes straight!

*Chuck Smith, Jr., the pastor of Calvary Chapel Capo Beach [California] and son of the pastor of the Calvary Chapel in Costa Mesa, a kind of "mother church" to the new worship movement in Southern California, details how the thorough freshness of the worship at Wimber's church compelled him to push further in musical reform in his home congregation. Smith's comments make the best sense when one remembers that some "traditional" elements sometimes characterized Calvary Chapel services, e.g., hymns carefully selected for thematic connection to the topic of the sermon in Costa Mesa's Sunday morning service.[23] Smith's recollections highlight a difficulty in studying this congregation: While he can describe the dynamism felt during this church's worship, a reader must imagine what it felt and sounded like.*

Smith desires to replicate his experience of true worship. Remember Wimber's pastoral awareness of the possible manipulative power of music. How can worshipers discern the difference between being moved merely by the music and being moved by God?

The singing began with "Well, Don't You Know It's Time to Praise the Lord?"[24] Immediately everyone was on their feet. The first few songs were completely new to me, but I enjoyed them. They were lyrics of love and devotion sung directly to God or Jesus, and the music sounded very contemporary (not rock, but adult contemporary). There was so much enthusiasm among those who sang that it felt contagious. I worshiped God that night. A week earlier I could not even define worship or describe what it looked like. But that night I worshiped; I was one to one with Jesus, telling Him I loved Him, adored Him, that He is truly awesome, and I was grateful for His love and sacrifice for me. I left CCYL [Calvary Chapel Yorba Linda, the Anaheim Vineyard's original location, affiliation, and name] that night in a state of "spiritual mourning" that lasted for several days, because I felt, by comparison, our church was dead. The life of the Spirit in worship was definitely not with us. So we made immediate changes.

*Music was an important part of Vineyard worship from the beginning for the entire congregation. Here are several reminisces on this early music, the first from Cheryl Pittluck, wife of the current Anaheim Vineyard senior pastor.[25]*

The songs were simple and easy to learn . . . no words on a screen or anything, so they had to be. I remember that it was so different from anything I'd seen or experienced. . . . I remember

23. Charles E. Fromm, "Textual Communities and New Song in the Multimedia Age: The Routinization of Charisma in the Jesus Movement" (Ph.D. diss., Fuller Theological Seminary, 2006), 270-71.

24. The song "Don't You Know It's Time to Praise the Lord" was written by Bruce and Judi Borneman and copyrighted in 1981 by Maranatha! Music. This song is an example of the use of Psalm 22:3 ("Thou inhabitest the praises of Israel" in the King James Version) and Old Testament passages to develop a theology in which God comes and is present as the church praises him. This theology was widespread in Pentecostal circles in the late twentieth century.

25. Cheryl Pittluck, electronic mail to Cindy Rethmeier, May 19, 2006.

John [Wimber] leading from the piano and his voice was so smooth and easy to follow . . . no showmanship, no performance . . . it just blended in with our voices. I remember that it was the best part of the service . . . the worship.

*Carol Wimber describes the importance of singing to God:*[26]

Worship was perhaps the first thing God told us to do and then He had to teach us how. . . . This was revolutionary to us: singing songs straight to Jesus. We sang love songs to Jesus, and it was this intimacy that broke us down. . . .

You can still keep a certain reserve intact singing theological songs about the faith. These songs are wonderful and I'm thankful for every one of them. But when you sing "You Bless Me, Lord, Forever" or "Whom Have I But You?",[27] it breaks through to your inner being and expresses what your spirit needs to say.

It wasn't everyone's cup of tea, of course. Much of the church was not comfortable with such deep intimacy, but we were instructed by the Lord to worship Him this way: "Sing to Him, sing praise to Him" (1 Chronicles 16:9).

We would worship God for a long time, as long as we wanted, wherever we wanted; we would worship first, and we would worship at the end. A meeting of two or three was reason to worship, and we worshiped in the airport on our way to bring a worship team to another country and many a times we got in trouble because we were late for meetings because the team was worshiping.

We worshiped God because He is worthy. To worship is the only adequate response to who Jesus is and what He has done for us. . . .

*Bev Martin's testimony of attending Anaheim Vineyard as a teen mixes a sense of the Holy Spirit's power and presence in worship with the importance of congregational singing in Vineyard worship. Notice how her background in the ecumenical Charismatic Movement gave her ways to appreciate the Vineyard's worship ministry.*[28]

My first encounter with the power of the Holy Spirit was not at the Vineyard, but rather, at a Holy Spirit Seminar in the Charismatic Movement of St. Norbert's Catholic Church. I was a Junior in high school. I attended a conference and was amazed by what happened. People were moving in the Holy Spirit in a powerful way. As they prayed over me, I immediately

Jesus is the recipient of worship. This emphasis follows a longstanding tendency in worship among evangelicals to focus devotionally on Jesus Christ as the object of worship, not solely as the mediator of worship to God the Father. Not surprisingly, the majority of the most-used "contemporary" songs for the last several years have made Jesus Christ, not God the Father, the primary recipient of worship.

26. John Wimber, *The Way In Is the Way On* (Atlanta: Ampelon Publishing, 2006), 108-9.

27. Carol Wimber is referring to two recent Vineyard songs: "You Bless Me, Lord" by Scott Underwood, copyright 1997 Mercy/Vineyard Publishing (Admin. by Vineyard Music USA), and "Whom Have I But You" by Luis Ruis, copyright 1996 Mercy/Vineyard Publishing (Admin. by Vineyard Music USA).

28. Bev Martin, electronic mail to Cindy Rethmeier, May 23, 2006.

began speaking and singing in tongues. People were prophesying, moving in healing, and falling under the power of the Spirit.

After the conference, I began going to Catholic charismatic prayer meetings. I remember praying in my car, "Lord, I feel like I have known you all my life. Now, I know your presence. Just in case, I give my life to you now!" It seems that it was only a matter of weeks before the priest at St. Norbert's shut down the Charismatic Movement. It caused a horrible and painful division for many Catholic believers who felt forced to leave the Catholic Church. At the time, I was 17 years old, the oldest of 5 siblings and a member of a truly Christian and devoted Catholic family. I felt very alone and unable to leave the church at that time.

Miraculously, in this time of pain, some of my high school friends invited me to a small gathering of believers meeting in a choir room at El Dorado High School on Sunday evenings. At the first meeting I went to, there was a man kneeling on stage, crying and begging the Holy Spirit to come upon us in power. His name was John Wimber. I fell in love with his sweet spirit that night and his yearning for more of the Holy Spirit. From my brief but powerful encounter with the Holy Spirit at St. Norbert's, I knew what he was longing for.

The Lord did answer John's prayer. Those early meetings were a time in history that the Lord's presence was overwhelming. We sang beautiful songs of praise as we adored and worshiped our Savior intimately. The power of the Spirit came and touched His people. It was evident that a movement of God was happening. People began to come. Soon we were meeting at Canyon High School, and we had become a church.

There were two key elements of the Vineyard that opened up people's hearts to experience intimacy with God. John Wimber described worship as "kissing the face of Jesus." We did not just sing, but rather, we worshiped the Almighty! We sang love songs to Jesus on our knees, with our hands held high. We were praying praises as we sang. It was as though we were singing with the angels in heaven in the throne room!

*In a 1983 sermon Wimber described the reason why the congregation used songs in a "contemporary idiom" rather than older hymns.*[29]

. . . the first thing the Lord called us to was to worship. And this church began with a group of people meeting in a home and learning to worship the Lord in much the same way that you heard this morning. From time to time I will have people visit, and they will say, 'Why don't you sing more of the old traditional hymns?' My response is that the Lord has called us to develop a new liturgy. With it we have had hundreds [of songs] that have either been written by people here in the fellowship, as many of the ones that we sang today were, or have been brought to us by other brethren that have had great meaning to us. So we are attempting

29. From a presentation entitled "Call to Missions" in "Basic Priorities of Vineyard Christian Fellowship," Box 13, John Wimber Collection, Regent University Library Archives, Virginia Beach, Virginia, 1-2.

---

*Margin notes:*

Notice how this worshiper understood in cultural images of romance Wimber's teaching on certain biblical words for worship.

In his ministry, John Wimber worked to clear up this misinterpretation. Upon further research of the word *proskuneo*, he found that a more accurate translation would be "kissing the feet of Jesus."

This dedication to being moved by the Lord to do something in worship could derive from either Quaker or Pentecostal roots. How dependent upon the Spirit's active guidance should worship planners and leaders be in the specifics of a service?

to worship in a contemporary idiom in order to express our love to God, and to do it in language that suits us and music that [is] appropriate to our tastes. This is not in any way negative about what God is doing in other fellowship[s] and the importance of heritage and the importance of the great old anthems and hymns. I frankly like many of them, love them, occasionally want to sing them, but never feel moved by the Lord to sing them. I feel that we are doing what we are supposed to do. I suppose if nobody was singing them, I would really be disturbed.

## Worshipers Describe the Dramatic Ministry of the Holy Spirit during Worship

*Vineyard worshipers saw the Holy Spirit move during worship. Cindy Rethmeier explains how the gifts of the Holy Spirit worked hand-in-hand with the musical worship.*

Often John [Wimber] would spend the whole worship time looking out over the congregation as he played keys, and then he would begin telling us things God had shown him about people in the congregation. He didn't usually point certain people out and give the word directly at them—he would tell what he "saw in his mind's eye." He called this kind of revelation "word of knowledge." We understood that as we worshiped, the presence of God came and gifts were released. We didn't worship so that gifts would be released. Rather, the gifts were the overflow of time spent before God, worshiping him. . . .

*Healing of emotional pain was another common occurrence as the Holy Spirit fell upon the congregation. Cindy Rethmeier describes one occurrence for her husband, Steve.*

One night during worship, I noticed tears on Steve's face as we were worshiping. Afterwards he described how he had, seemingly out of no where, remembered a painful experience. During worship it was as if God had taken him back to the memory and had healed him from the pain of the memory. Healing of memories, physical healing, deliverance and salvation all began occurring spontaneously during worship, *before* the teaching or ministry time. God was on the move!

*Mary Guleserian portrays how her deep personal need, the Lord's healing hand, small group meetings, and the loving ministry of early Vineyard participants combined to provide her with an answer to prayer and a new Christian home for worship.*[30]

30. Mary Guleserian, electronic mail to Cindy Rethmeier, May 21, 2006.

Charismatic and Pentecostal Christians were attentive to the lists of the gifts (*charismata* in Greek) of the Spirit as found in Scripture. Such lists are found in Romans 12, Ephesians 4, and 1 Corinthians 12.

So powerful were the times of extended singing that "worship" became practically synonymous with making music to the Lord. Rethmeier's testimony highlights the major sections of a common order of worship in this type of congregation: extended worship (singing), biblical teaching, and concluding time of prayer ("ministry time").

What can I tell you about those glorious days of the beginning of the Vineyard back at Canyon High School? I was such a new Christian, just a few years old in the Lord. I started going to the Vineyard because my pastor, Lance Pittluck,[31] and his wife, my best friend, Cheryl, started going Sunday evenings.

Cheryl and I had a friend, Linda, who'd had a spinal fusion. She'd been a dancer and majored in college in dance. Dance was her life, her passion. Months after her surgery, she tried to dance again, but unfortunately she got a new fracture in her spine. Linda was in terrible pain and was facing surgery again.

Cheryl and Lance took her to the Vineyard. They were totally into what was going on there. We were clueless.

A little back-story before I go on. At nineteen I gave up a son for adoption. Then at twenty-two, I married and had a son, Joel. But my dreams ended when my husband left me for another woman.

Four years after I married my second husband, Armen, I suffered through two back-to-back miscarriages. I was miserable.

After Lance and Cheryl took my friend Linda that Sunday for prayer, Linda and Cheryl called me a few days later. They told me that Linda had been healed! They'd had an x-ray that showed Linda's fracture. And now the new x-ray showed no fracture. Cheryl also told me of other things that were happening at the Vineyard. I said to myself, "Hey! I want some of that!" My dream of having a child with my husband was very important to me.

We started going to church with Lance and Cheryl in the evenings, and we loved it. The worship was outstanding, and so new and glorious for us both. I went to the Wagner house for Bible study, and women's groups. My OBGYN had just prescribed a drug to make me produce more eggs. I was very uncomfortable on this drug and felt a bit sick.

On a Sunday at evening service, a woman came up to me out of the blue. I have no idea who she was, and to this day, don't know. She looked a little uneasy and finally just said to me, "Look, the Lord wants you off that medicine you're on." She gave me a funny, "Whew, okay, I said it," look. I said to her. "Okay! I understand." I was thrilled beyond belief. God was looking out for me! I had no idea what else he had planned, but I wanted more of Him.

Because the Wagner house offices were very close to where we women were hanging out during Bible study, Bob Fulton overheard me telling someone about this woman. He said, "What is it that you want?" I said, "Oh, I've had two miscarriages, and I'm trying to get pregnant, and I'm not having any success" . . . and told him about the woman at Canyon High School.

He said, "I want to pray for you." Embarrassed by all the attention I'd garnered for myself, I said with a decisive nod, "Great, thanks. I appreciate it." And I turned away. Bob reached out

John Wimber summarizes the way that "power from on high" is experienced in the congregation: "Today, our large and small gatherings are characterized by things that I had known about only from history books. Quaking, shaking, falling under the power of God, and the public exercise of spiritual gifts, such as words of knowledge and prophecy, are commonplace." Source: John Wimber, "Zip to 3,000 in 5 Years," *Christian Life* 44, no. 6 (October 1982): 21.

31. Lance Pittluck has been the pastor of the Anaheim Vineyard congregation from 1997 to the present.

and said, "No, now." He called the women together and about six of us trooped upstairs to a room at the Wagner house. I was so mortified and appalled, truly. I laugh to think about it now; that I was humiliated and embarrassed by what the Lord would do for *me*. I was nobody. I had no idea what God would do. But remember, I was a baby Christian and not at all familiar with my faith. And I certainly did not know what I believed.

That day, those five women and Bob anointed my head with oil and prayed over me. I didn't feel a thing. I didn't feel the Spirit, nothing. I so just wanted to go out to my car and get that olive oil off me. That's how ignorant I was. Good thing we have a God who is far, far more awesome than we give Him credit for. I like to think He chuckled over my idiocy.

But here's the thing. Because of my new faith, my baby steps, my brokenness, the thing that became the most important to me was seeking the face of God . . . [and] having a child wasn't the number one issue any longer. It wasn't about me.

Now, what was important was knowing Jesus Christ, who chose me. He wanted me on His team. And I was willing to play! I began to earnestly seek God. I joined Bible studies, we hosted a Kinship [small group meeting], and we had people over every Tuesday night from the Vineyard and other churches, all who wanted to experience the power of God's Holy Spirit. It was an awesome time.

On Sundays following my anointing, I felt I was to wait on the Lord. I'd sit in the bleachers at the High School and weep at reciting out loud from Psalm 127:3–5: "Sons are a heritage from the Lord, children are a reward from him," which I thrillingly took to heart. One evening John Wimber read Psalm 139:13–16, "For you created my inmost being; you knit me together in my mother's womb. I praise you because I am fearfully and wonderfully made . . . my frame was not hidden from you when I was made in the secret place. When I was woven together in the depths of the earth, your eyes saw my unformed body . . ." I was struck speechless reading these words along with John. I felt the Lord speaking to me, and I wept in sheer gratitude that he'd heard my cry.

In the warm evenings up in the bleachers, I'd sit in worship and I'd get this picture of myself pregnant. Delighted, I'd open my eyes, and a pregnant woman walked by, right in front of me. I felt God was preparing me. Then I'd play a game. I'd shut my eyes and turn to the right and wait awhile and then open my eyes and there was another pregnant woman sitting across from me. Or again, I'd shut my eyes while the music played and turn to the opposite direction, and wait until I could stand it no longer, open my eyes, and see a pregnant woman on her way to the restrooms. I felt God was telling me, "it's going to happen . . . but on my terms." I'd been off the drug the doctor had prescribed for about six to eight weeks, and I started feeling normal again.

I was a few weeks late with my period, and I just knew, I just knew that I was pregnant. But most of all, I knew that I wasn't going to miscarry. I was sure of it. So I decided to go and get a pregnancy test the following Monday.

One of the appealing (or, perhaps to some, frightening) things about Charismatic (and Pentecostal) spirituality and worship is the intense sense of the immediacy of God's presence. Rather than being a generic, faraway God worshiped by generic worshipers in abstraction, God is intimately connected to worshipers.

The Friday before, I was doing a quiet Bible study in my bed late at night, reading over scripture and meditating on God's Word. It was time for me to turn out the light and I reached up and clicked the lamp off. Moonlight streamed in, and I closed my eyes. I said, in my head to God, "You know, [and] I know I'm pregnant, and You know I'm going to go have that pregnancy test on Monday . . . but I would like for YOU to tell me that I'm pregnant." And without any warning, three pictures came to me. They were living pictures of an embryo whose heart was beating. And these three distinct pictures were at different angles, clear, concise and brilliant. Bam. Bam. Bam. And I knew. I was thrilled in my heart of hearts; I knew that was my child. For months afterward, I tried to recreate those pictures in my head. I was unable to do it. They were a gift from God. Twenty-three years ago, I was given the miracle of relying on my Savior, trusting in him, waiting on Him, and was given the thing my heart had yearned for.

*In a series of presentations on the priorities of the Vineyard given in 1983, John Wimber launched into reminiscing from time to time on the journey that the congregation had taken since its start. In the following passage, Wimber hints at the increasing Pentecostal/Charismatic nature of the congregation's worship, which was not always comfortable to experience, even for members.*[32]

Wimber is likely speaking about singing in tongues (glossolalia).

A few years ago when God began ministering to us, I can remember the first occasion which the Holy Spirit spoke to me and said, "Lead out **singing in the Spirit** in the congregation." That was about three and a half years ago. Well, the Bibles slammed, and doors slammed, people got up and left. They were angry. I got phone calls and letters over the next few days. "Show me where that is in the Bible!" I didn't know it at the time, but I do now. But I didn't know what they were talking about. All that I knew was that they were grumpy and angry at me. All I was doing was what God told me to do. They didn't ask me, "Did God tell you to do that?" They just said, "Show me in the Bible!" A few months later God began speaking to me about healing. We would lay hands on some people and try to heal them. I would say, "I think it is the Word here that God wants to heal people." People would be looking at each other, "Do you believe him?" "I don't believe him." "He's always telling us these things." I remember that was a "biggie." I almost got run out of town over that one. "Who me?" It was fun. It wasn't really all that much fun to tell the truth. But it was OK. It was part of growing up a church. God began manifesting Himself in power in the church. I got a lot of phone calls on that one. "What was that guy doing up there?" "I don't know. I didn't put him up there." "Why was he there?" "Well, because God did that." You know sometimes when God comes to church He acts like God. He does just whatever He wants to do without asking permission.

We went through all kinds of dialogue. Most of that is out of the way now. In recent times

32. From a presentation entitled "Fellowship" in "Basic Priorities of Vineyard Christian Fellowship," Box 13, John Wimber Collection, Regent University Library Archives, Virginia Beach, Virginia, 18-20.

God has been moving with such incredible power in the church that we have seen manifestations of all kinds of things, some of them hard to explain. I haven't had to explain them to too many because we have been too busy being joyful that they are happening, to see a people that have learned to come to the party. That is a people that have been learning to enjoy the things of the Spirit. . . .

In more recent times He has been ministering to the demonized and that was a tough one. The first time I met a demon I didn't like him. I have never met a demon I like so far. I don't know anybody who likes them. I don't think they like themselves. Sometimes they do crazy things. I thank God that He is freeing people of them and of the work they do, the terrible, terrible work of destruction.

I took inventory the other day, the only thing left is raising the dead. We have seen everything else. The Holy Spirit spoke to me the other day and He said, "You are going to see that. It is coming. Just keep on truckin'." Learn the Word, learn to do, because you don't get there in one giant step. Maturity doesn't happen overnight. It takes time. We must learn to trust and love one another, even as we learn to trust Him if we are to grow into a Body that will see the dead raised. I believe that is what is going to happen. I have been asking the Lord to hold off for a while. "Don't come back too soon, Jesus. Do this first, cause us to become a people that are one in you." Amen.

*Carol Wimber describes an example of the Holy Spirit's anointing for worship, evidenced by a gift of song given to a boy and a powerful healing. The scene is from England, an early instance of the spread of the Vineyard's ministry.*[33]

. . . We brought the first ministry team of teenagers to St. Michael's Le'Belfrey in York, England. It was 1981. John and I had been praying together for the meeting that evening when the Lord gave me a word from 2 Chronicles 29:27–28:

> Then Hezekiah gave the order to sacrifice the burnt offering on the altar. As the offering began, singing to the Lord began also, accompanied by trumpets and the instruments of David king of Israel. The whole assembly bowed in worship, while the singers sang and the trumpeters played. All this continued until the sacrifice of the burnt offering was finished.

John would always refer to this word as "the time in York when God gave him that word." However it happened, that evening the Holy Spirit began to move in a tremendously powerful way. Blind eyes saw, the deaf ears heard, and the lame walked. The whole while a young boy sang in the influence of the Spirit. A boy around 13 or 14 years old was just standing there

---

33. Carol Wimber, "The Flame of God's Presence," in John Wimber, *The Way In Is the Way On* (Atlanta: Ampelon Publishing, 2006), 106-7.

Compare Jesus's testimony to that of John the Baptist in Matthew 11:5. Seeing a continuation of God demonstrating miraculous powers between biblical times and now is often an important aspect of a Charismatic worldview.

when the Holy Spirit fell. The Spirit fell on him and he raised up his head and began to sing in the Spirit. He continued singing without a pause for the entire hour or so that the Lord was manifesting His presence with signs, wonders, and healings. He didn't stop singing until it was all done. John and I understood that night, that for us, the Vineyard, that song and singing would always be attached to the presence and manifestation of the Holy Spirit.

## Reports on Worship from Early Church Planters

*Even in its earliest days the Anaheim congregation spawned church planters who went out and started new Vineyard churches. As they did so, these planters carried with them the seeds of a Vineyard way of worship, first across the United States and then around the world. For example, note how the 1984 description from worshipers in the initial church plant by Todd and Debbie Hunter in Wheeling, West Virginia, sounds like it could have described the Anaheim home church.*[34]

A sense of God's presence, authenticity, healing, and fellowship are the qualities of Vineyard worship and life identified in this report. Do Americans still seek the same in churches today? Does the desire for these qualities arise out of the New Testament description of the church or out of American cultural sensibilities? Or could it be both?

The privilege of worshiping at the Vineyard is truly an answer to prayer. As we walked closer and closer to the Lord, we had a deep desire to experience worship in a way that was not possible in the church we had been attending for many years. We desired to come into God's presence and "be there" with Him. Worship at the Vineyard has given us this wonderful opportunity. At each service we are touched by the Spirit of the Living God. We are refreshed, revived, cleansed, healed, delivered, corrected, and blessed abundantly. We always leave (but nobody really wants to leave after the service is over) knowing that we have truly been in God's presence and have experienced his love, grace, mercy and tender touch.

At last we could be "ourselves." We could take off the masks! At the Vineyard we found that everybody was accepted and loved and there was no need to "fit into the mold."

We have found a place to both give and receive. It is beautiful to watch God at work through his servants as people minister to each other's needs, as they pray for the healing of bodies, relationships, jobs and families. There is never a reason to go home without knowing that God and his people really care and are willing to listen and help.

In just the few weeks since our new Kinship group was formed, we have grown to truly and deeply love the people God has gathered. We anxiously look forward to Thursday evening and being together for intimate fellowship, worship, and sharing and praying for our friends.

We thank God for his generous gift to us—a place of worship which satisfies our souls—and which, I know, pleases his as well.

---

34. Grace and Marc Dallanegra, "Touched by the Spirit," *First Fruits* (June 1984): 13.

*Gerald Martinez, a Vineyard church planter in Durango, Colorado, was interviewed for the September 1984 issue of the denominational magazine,* First Fruits. *In the interview Martinez stated that worship was his congregation's first priority.*[35] *He also argued for the necessity of the church to adapt to meet the needs of contemporary culture. This line of thought became a common one as mainline churches began intentionally to adopt new forms of worship in the 1990s.*

Q. Why did you start another church when Durango already has 30 churches?

A. Because there are unsaved people looking to be accepted and loved. These people are looking for a church that will meet their needs. They have seen the traditional church and have rejected it. They need an alternative and we believe God will provide that with the Vineyard.

Q. What are your priorities as a church?

A. Our first priority is WORSHIP. I believe that worship is a key ingredient in bringing people in contact with God. Our church wants to be known as a church that truly worships God in spirit and in truth. Our plans are to develop worship teams and ministry teams in the area of drama, dance, and music. Worship is a key ingredient in our relationship to God. This is one thing the Vineyard has really helped us with, and the one thing that people most comment about. Our second priority is FELLOWSHIP. This is what relates a brother to a brother and sister to a sister, and together they can become the Body of Christ. Our third priority is EVANGELISM. Jesus came to seek and save the lost. This is what the ministry is all about. Our fourth priority is TRAINING ministers. My desire is to establish ministries in this community and in the community abroad.

> The pastor speaks of drama and dance teams; these are changes from worship in the early Anaheim Vineyard.

Q. Why do you think Vineyard is different than many of the other churches today?

A. I believe that much of what we see today in the church was born during the Reformation and was contemporary to its culture. Today we live in a culture that has progressed and developed faster than any other culture on the earth. The church has failed to penetrate our contemporary society. Vineyard is a ministry, in my estimation, that has begun to relate to our society and to its needs. The Bible speaks of new wine-skins, and says that you can't put new wine in old wine-skins. People today can relate to the ministry of the Vineyard, because it is new, and yet true to God's Word. The worship is new and exciting, [and] the ministry of the Spirit is fresh and realistic. This is what people are looking for. John Wimber said that people don't have a problem with Jesus; they have a problem with the church, so the church needs to change. We need to relate to our culture in terms that they can understand.

> Although Martinez does not use the term "contemporary worship," he does speak of contemporary culture or society. Within ten years mainline churches began to address this desire to have forms of worship that fit "contemprary" culture. Given these dynamics—and the already existing term "contemporary Christian music"—was it inevitable that someone would eventually coin the phrase "contemporary worship"?

35. "Church Planting: An Interview with Gerald Martinez," *First Fruits* (September 1984): 9, 14.

# ORDER OF SERVICE AND TEXTS

## A Representative Song

*The role that congregational songs played in connecting worshipers to God cannot be overstated. "You Are Here" is a good example of the type of songs the Vineyard worshipers sang. This song begins with a direct address to God ("You") that relishes God's presence in worship, common in Vineyard worship. The melody is characteristically simple with a limited range of notes. These features enhance congregational singing by freeing worshipers from worrying about the technical aspects of singing and, instead, allowing them to focus on the Lord, the recipient of worship. Since the church did not provide the lyrics to worshipers by either a bulletin or projection, simple lyrics helped congregational singing, too. This song, copyrighted in 1985, also helped Vineyard spark a surge of worship songwriting that still continues.*

Source: "You Are Here." Words and music by Patty Kennedy-Marine. The song was published in *Songs of the Vineyard*, vol. 4, copyright 1985 by Vineyard Ministries International and Mercy Records. © 1985 Mercy/Vineyard Publishing (Admin. by Vineyard Music USA). Used with permission.

## *Some Songs Written by John Wimber*

*Early Vineyard worship was caught up in the surge of songwriting that marked the California worship movements of the 1970s. The phenomenon has not waned as "contemporary worship" has grown and expanded. John Wimber himself contributed to the songs for the Anaheim Vineyard congregation, although he was by no means the only contributor to that congregation's expanding song repertoire. The following two songs exemplify Wimber's versatility. The first, "Sweet Perfume," uses a motif common in Wimber's ministry of how God's love can reach the brokenhearted. The second, "Together," rejoices in the unity Christians share in God. Both songs also demonstrate that, even with the Vineyard's emphasis on singing to the Lord, songs that explored other dimensions of worship and church life also were embraced. The following two songs are both exhortations sung to fellow worshipers.*

**Sweet Perfume**

Verse 1:  Consider how He loves you,
              His arms of love enfold you,
              Like a sweet, sweet perfume.

Verse 2:  He left His word to guide us,
              His presence lives inside us,
              Like a sweet, sweet perfume.

Chorus:  Don't ever think that you're worthless,
              You have His life within.
              You are a sweet, wholesome fragrance,
              So valuable, to Him.

Verse 3:  He'll light up all your darkness,
              And fill you with His Spirit
              Like a sweet, sweet perfume.

The image of perfume is not only easily understood within the culture, but has several biblical resonances (see 2 Corinthians 2:15 and John 12:3). The Bible uses the image of perfume in terms of God's transformation of a person in Christ and of tender adoration of God.

Verse 4:  Your prayers are very precious,

They reach the heart of Jesus

Like a sweet, sweet perfume.

**Together**

Verse 1:  I am yours *(echo: I am yours)*,

You are mine *(You are mine)*,

We are one *(We are one)*.

With the Father *(with the Father)*,

In the Spirit *(in the Spirit)*,

By the Son *(by the Son)*.

Such an explicitly Trinitarian song is unusual within the larger body of "contemporary" worship songs, both then and now. It is also unusual for this music to speak about church issues like unity.

Chorus:  And we know that we will always be together.

Through all eternity, together.

Verse 2:  Jesus You *(Jesus You)*

Are the Lord *(are the Lord)*

Of us all *(of us all)*.

You are here *(You are here)*,

Always near *(always near)*,

When we call *(when we call)*.

Chorus:  And we know that we will always be together.

Through all eternity, together.

Verse 3:  Brothers and *(brothers and)*

Sisters, we *(sisters, we)*

Are all one *(are all one)*.

With the Father *(with the Father)*,

In the Spirit *(in the Spirit)*,

By the Son *(by the Son)*.

Chorus:  And we know that we will always be together.

Through all eternity, together.

Source: "Sweet Perfume" was published in *Songs of the Vineyard*, vol. 1. "Together" was published in *Songs of the Vineyard: Just like You Promised*. Both bear 1982 copyrights by Vineyard Ministries International and Mercy Publishing. Both were eventually published together in *Worship Songs of the Vineyard* (Anaheim, CA: Vineyard Ministries International, 1989). "Sweet Perfume" appeared on the first Vineyard album, *All the Earth Shall Worship*, released in 1982. Used with permission.

## Anaheim Vineyard's Song Repertoire

*One of the marks of worship seen in the testimonies above was often the participant's appreciation of the new songs that were used. The following images show the table of contents of a collection of chord charts used by the musicians in the mid-1980s. Some are written by members of the congregation, and some come from other churches who were "singing a new song unto the Lord." Many of the songs come from Maranatha! Music, associated with the Calvary Chapel movement.*

*Some became some of the most used songs across "contemporary worship" even to the present day. The chord chart for one of the songs in the collection, "Spirit Song," written by John Wimber in the late 1970s, is included.*

TABLE OF CONTENTS                Page No.                                              Page No.

| | | | | |
|---|---|---|---|---|
| All Hail, King Jesus | 11 | | Jesus What A Wonder You Are | 65 |
| All That I Can Do Is Thank You | 26 | | John 16:33 | 56 |
| Amen, Praise the Lord | 1 | | Joshua 24:15 | 25 |
| Behold What Manner of Love | 38 | | Kingdom of Children | 31 |
| Bless Thou The Lord | 10 | | Let All That Is Within Me | 41 |
| Cause Me to Come | 3 | | Let's Forget About Ourselves | 4 |
| Charity | 5 | | Let's Just Praise The Lord | 84 |
| Christ in Me | 73 | | Love | 75 |
| Clay Vessell | 6 | | Love, Him | 68 |
| Come To The Cross | 59 | | Love , Love, Love | 27 |
| Come To The Water | 83 | | Matthew 16:24 | 82 |
| Father, I adore You | 55 | | More of Thee | 30 |
| Freely, Freely | 51 | | My Peace | 67 |
| Galations 2:20 | 22 | | O Come Let Us Adore Him | 32 |
| Hallelujah! | 80 | | Open My Eyes, Lord | 57 |
| Happy, Happy! | 7 | | Our God Reigns | 35 |
| Happy In Jesus | 53 | | Pass It On | 76 |
| He Died On The Cross | 79 | | Psalm 25 | 34 |
| He Is Exalted | 8 | | Psalm 34:1-4 | 16 |
| He Is Here | 12 | | Psalm 100 | 36 |
| He Is Lord | 15 | | Psalm 139:23-24 | 37 |
| He Touched Me | 64 | | Psalm 148 | 40 |
| He Will Rise Again | 18 | | Praise Him | 61 |
| Holy Father | 71 | | Praise Song | 42 |
| Holy, Holy, Holy | 47 | | Right On Relationship | 44 |
| Holy, Thou Art Holy | 19 | | Savior of My Soul | 28 |
| Humble Thyself | 86 | | Seek Ye First | 45 |
| I Cast My Cares Upon You | 60 | | Set My Spirit Free | 2 |
| I Keep Falling In Love | 21 | | Shepherd's Song | 33 |
| I Live | 43 | | Since I've Opened Up | 46 |
| I Love You Lord | 14 | | Something Beautiful | 69 |
| I See The Lord | 78 | | Spirit Song | 48 |
| Jesus | 39 | | Sweet Sweet Spirit | 74 |
| Jesus I Love You | 66 | | Thank You | 72 |
| Jesus Is The One | 20 | | Thank You, Lord | 29 |
| Jesus My Lord | 24 | | The Greatest Thing | 13 |
| Jesus Name Above All Names | 62 | | The Love Of My Lord | 70 |

TABLE OF CONTENTS Continued     Page No.

| | |
|---|---|
| The Lord of the Dance | 49 |
| There's Something About That Name | 77 |
| This Is My Commandment | 50 |
| Thou Shalt Love The Lord Thy God | 81 |
| Two Hands | 63 |
| Thy Loving Kindness | 52 |
| Trust In His Love | 85 |
| Turn Your Eyes Upon Jesus | 54 |
| You Are My Goodness | 9 |
| Walking In The Will | 58 |
| We are gathering Together | 17 |
| Zephaniah 3:17 | 23 |

SPIRIT SONG                                    (48)

```
     D    D7          G         Em
1.  O LET THE SON OF GOD ENFOLD YOU
                   F#m7
    WITH HIS SPIRIT AND HIS LOVE
           G
    LET HIM FILL YOUR HEART
          A7        D
    AND SATISFY YOUR SOUL
     D    D7      G
    O LET HIM HAVE THE THINGS THAT
     Em          F#m7       Bm7
    HOLD YOU - AND HIS SPIRIT LIKE A DOVE
          G         A7
    WILL DESCEND UPON YOUR LIFE AND MAKE
          G     D
    YOU WHOLE.

            G   A7   F#m7   Bm7   A7     D
    (CHORUS) JESUS, O JESUS  COME AND TAKE YOUR LAMB
            G   A7   F#m7   Bm7   A7   G  D
    JESUS, O JESUS,  COME AND TAKE YOUR LAMB

2.  O COME AND SING THIS SONG WITH GLADNESS
    AS YOUR HEARTS ARE FILLED WITH JOY
    LIFT YOUR HANDS IN SWEET SURRENDER
    TO HIS NAME
    O GIVE HIM ALL YOUR TEARS AND SADNESS
    GIVE HIM ALL YOUR YEARS OF PAIN
    AND YOU'LL ENTER INTO LIFE IN JESUS' NAME.

    (CHORUS) ............. COME AND FILL YOUR LAMB
    (CHORUS) ............. COME AND HEAL YOUR LAMB
```

Source: The table of contents was scanned from the original notebook-bound collection. "Spirit Song" is copyrighted 1979 by Mercy Records/Vineyard Publishing and administered by Music Services, Inc. Used by permission: Sean and Christy Wimber, 2015 @ Yorba Linda Vineyard/Wimber. Global.

## Songs from the 1982 Album

*In 1982, after John Wimber decided that the music of the congregation needed to be documented, a studio album was cut and released.[1] It was entitled* All the Earth Shall Worship *after one of the congregation's songs on the album. Most of the musicians were studio artists, although the songs on the album were mainly compositions by members of the church's worship team: Carl Tuttle, John Wimber, and Eddie Espinosa. A picture of the congregation in the Canyon High School gymnasium appeared on the back cover. From this point forward the cultivation of new songs, their recording, and their distribution would be part of the Vineyard's national and, eventually, international influence. Ten songs appeared on this initial album:*

**Side A**

Exodus XV (words and music by Frank Gallian)

I Worship You (words and music by Carl Tuttle)

I Sing a New Song (words and music by Carl Tuttle and John Wimber)

Holy Is the Lord (words and music by Brian L. Beshears)

The Lord God Most High (words and music by Carl Tuttle)

**Side B**

Closer to Thee (words and music by Eddie Espinosa)

I Only Want to Love You (words and music by Eddie Espinosa)

Sweet Perfume (words and music by John Wimber)

All the Earth Shall Worship (words and music by Carl Tuttle)

Alleluia (words and music by Carl Tuttle)

---

1. Carl Tuttle, telephone interview by Lester Ruth, February 1, 2013.

# SERMONS

## John Wimber's Sermon on "Loving God"

*Concerned that the real heart of worship might be missed or that worship might be misunderstood, John Wimber often preached to teach Vineyard worshipers about the proper nature of worship. The following sermon, which dates from the late 1970s based on the clues Wimber gives at the beginning, describes Wimber's own sense of reluctance to what he first experienced in this new way of worship. Over the course of the sermon, he discusses a variety of topics to build a well-rounded biblical approach to worship. Worship is about a whole-hearted, whole-life affection for the Lord, and it is loving adoration of the One who has done so much for the worshiper. Of particular theological interest in the sermon is Wimber's discussion of the three dimensions of a human person and how worship relates to each. In addition, the Charismatic Movement's influence on the congregation is evident as Wimber teaches on what he considers the proper scriptural use of the gifts of the Spirit, including tongues. Many of the recurring qualities of Wimber's speaking are also evident in this sermon, including a sense of humor and a folksy style.*

Some of us had never worshiped much in our lives. I've been a Christian, I think, nearly sixteen years now [Wimber was converted in 1963], and I knew a little bit of worship. I'd had some glimpses of it from time to time, but I really didn't know what it entailed.

About a year and half ago I went to a gathering of this church before it was a church in a home. And they sat and sang in this house for an hour and a half, and then they sorta shared a little bit some verses, and then they prayed together. And frankly, I was sort of bored with the whole experience. I didn't really know what was happening. And I sat there. And I'm sure I was just a delight to everybody. I have a way of making my presence felt. And I didn't know what it was all about. And I remembered coming home, and Carol says, "What did you think of it?" She had been going for four, five weeks since it's been started.

It is intriguing to realize that this way of worship existed prior to Wimber's embracing of it. What this house church was experiencing was part of a larger phenomenon in Southern California at the time.

Wimber is showing self-deprecating humor, which he often did.

87

I said, "Gee, I don't know. I already know how to sing. And I know most of those songs, and I don't know. You know, what are you doing?"

She said, "That's what worship is."

I said, "Oh, yeah, I, uh, sure." I didn't know that there was a test going on. You know, sometimes you're in the midst of being tested, and you didn't even know it. And, in this particular case, I was being tested by God in a very interesting way.

In our society, you know, we have an emphasis on the gathering of knowledge and information, and we call that learning. But I really distinguish the gathering of information and understanding from learning in this sense. I think understanding is something that you acquire. Learning is something you learn to do. I can understand something and not have learned it in the sense that it is not working in my life. So I think learning has to do with behavior. Understanding has to do with the acquisition of information. Quite often I have information on something I had not learned. I had not learned to do. I had information on worship, but I had never learned how to worship. I see worship as a learned process, something that's really not natural to our culture. We really don't know much about worshiping.

Trying to develop some basic understanding of it, I came up with some Greek and Hebrew words that I won't try to pronounce. But basically worship comes down to four or five concepts that are repeated in different ways and in different places in scripture. And one of the key concepts in the Old Testament is to prepare a sacrifice. That is to say, you are worshiping when you are preparing a sacrifice. Another one is to adore, another one is to bow down, another one is to pay divine honor to. And we get in a sense that worship has to do with coming before God and giving yourself over to God.

Let's turn to Micah, the sixth chapter, if you can find Micah within two minutes, you're very spiritual. Ah, this is a little spirit check, a little reality check here to see just really, you know. Those of you . . . you can just really, you know, those of you—oh, you turned right to it, eh? Well, you can sit in the front row next week. Down here with Manuel, and he's the only one and he's still looking for it. It's in the Old Testament, Manuel, not the New Testament. Now if you had been raised in the synagogues in a typical orthodox Jewish community, you would know this text very well because it's one that's often recited in the worship services. And it's key to some very important understandings in the um, I turned to Malachi, what do you think of that? After [I was] hanging you up, Manuel. Here it is. It's key to understanding much of the Jewish tradition and much of the relationship between God and man generally. I'm going to begin with the sixth verse and read to the eighth.

With what shall I come to the Lord and bow myself before the God on high? Shall I come to him with burnt offerings, with yearling calves? Does the Lord take delight in thousands of rams, in ten thousand rivers of oil? Shall I present my first-born for my rebellious acts, the fruit

---

Such statements show how fundamental it was for many of these Vineyard worshipers to learn a new way to worship. Their "conversions" were not so much basic (becoming Christians) as finally tapping into a deeply meaningful, authentic approach to worshiping God.

Developing a theology of worship on the basis of biblical word studies seems to have been a method popular with Wimber and others.

of my body for the sin of my soul? He has told you, O man, what is good. And what does the Lord require of you but to do justice, to love kindness, and to walk humbly with your God?[1]

Now we have a contrast here between the sacrificial system that was given by God for the cleansing of sin and the sacrifice of a life and we see that even here in the Old Testament hidden, as it were, in the Minor Prophets is the understanding that God has always been after us, not after the things we do for him, not after the things we did for our sin, not after the sacrifices. He's been after us from the very beginning. And what he wants from you, what he wants from me is to walk humbly before him. That is to say, God wants our fellowship and our companionship.

Let's look in the New Testament to sorta tie this down with a cross reference: Romans 12: 1 and 2. Now Paul in the book of Romans teaches through the issues of sin and mankind generally. Here in the twelfth chapter he gets into some application as it relates to the teaching that he has given prior to this. And he says,

> I urge you, therefore, brethren, by the mercies of God to present your bodies as a living and holy sacrifice acceptable to God, which is your spiritual service of worship. And do not be conformed to this world, but be transformed by the renewing of your mind that you may prove what the will of God is, that which is good and acceptable and perfect.

The word "perfect" meaning complete. That is to say, that it is God's intention that we learn to worship him body, soul, and spirit. All three realms of our existence.

Just as God is a triune being—Father, Son, and Holy Spirit—we are a tripartite being which reflects the three part nature of God in that we have a body, soul, and spirit. Now sometime back I did a series on those and explained the realms and the way they work but, just for review, remember that the spirit is that inner person of your personality. That is the essence of you and your spirit. You were born with a spirit that needed to be regenerated, that needed to be renewed. Without that regeneration and renewal, you could never know God. And in the exchange that Jesus and Nicodemus had in the third chapter of John, we're taught that the Spirit of God moves on our spirit, and we become born again. That is a very popular phrase these days. You hear it applied to many things. But it basically means one thing: that when we were born the first time, we were born with a spirit that was destined to an eternity in hell. But because of the work of Jesus Christ through his death and resurrection, we have available to us a born again experience, a second birth. And I like that because one birth and one death is a wipe out, but two births and one death leaves an extra one, you know, and I needed an extra one. So I've been born again of the Spirit of God. That is to say, my spirit is rejuvenated when

In terms of a technical theological explanation of the Trinity, Wimber's analogy is not the best way of speaking; God's nature is three-Personed, not three-part. At a different level, however, the analogy is useful for being able to speak about different dimensions of a human (body, soul, and spirit) fitting together to form a unified whole. Wimber's ultimate point is an important one: Our worship of God must involve our whole persons in every dimension.

1. Here and throughout the sermon, Wimber is reading from the New American Standard Bible.

I receive Christ as my savior. Now the interesting thing is that I can be a born again person of God and still be living a pretty messed up life because I may not have come into obedience with the 12th chapter here of Romans. That is to say, I can be born again of the Spirit of God, receive the grace of God, and say, "Oh God, I do want to be saved. Oh God, I do want to be born again. Take my life" and then hedge at the point of really dedicating daily my body and my mind to the purposes of God.

That's what we're talking about here in Romans 12:1 and 2. He says to present your body as a living and holy sacrifice. Now that means daily giving your body and your mind to God so that the mind can be renewed and the body can be sacrificed. That's what Paul is talking about in 1 Corinthians, the second chapter when he talks to the Corinthians and he says, "You guys are still carnal-minded. I can't feed you adult food." And that word "carnal-minded" means body-ruled. Your body is still in control; you're still running on the same old fleshly appetites that you were running on before. Yes, you're born again of the Spirit of God, but you're still living like you weren't. You're still living with all the fleshly appetites you had before. You're running on the same fuel that you did before you were saved, before you were born again. So, the essence, the beginning of worship and the end of worship is for us to come into conformity to the will of God, which is, to give our body, soul, and spirit over to the adoration and to the love of God.

Now worship is not contained just in our meetings. Although in Hebrews—you might want to write some of this down for checking later—in Hebrews 10:25, we're admonished to assemble ourselves together. That is to say, "forget not the assembling of yourselves together." That is to say, it is essential for your growth and for mine that I gather in a group like this week after week. Somebody asked, "Why do I go to church?" I said, "Because I love it." If I didn't love it, I wouldn't go. When I didn't love it, I didn't go. And I wouldn't want anyone to come to this body if they didn't like it. Sometimes I see somebody come in under duress, their elbows still aching because their wife or their friend or somebody talked them into it. And I think, "That's all right for a one shot deal." You know, it's like trying yogurt for the first time, you know. My wife tells me everybody ought to eat yogurt once. I said, "Not if they have eyes, not if they can see it." That's the weirdest looking stuff I've ever seen. But she tells me, "You oughta try it once," and I think, "You oughta go to worship one time." And if you don't dig it, you know, don't go. My feeling is that, if it's not where you're at, it's not where you're at. So why play games with your mind? Why bring your body some place where your heart and mind isn't?

Frankly, it slows the worship down for other people if you have too many people whose hearts and bodies aren't, you know, there at one time. My perception is that worship is for the saints, worship is for those people who love God. I was talking to a guy Wednesday, having lunch with him, and he was telling about coming to church here. He said, "I don't wanna, you know, cast any negative thoughts your way or anything, but I really didn't get what . . . I

In this simple way, Wimber undercuts any suggestion that worship as seen from the pews should be a "spectator sport" where worshipers passively look on as someone worships for them in an entertaining way. To build on an analogy Wimber uses elsewhere: to allow someone to worship God for you, even if you enjoyed the experience, would be like hiring a substitute to love your spouse. Such spectator-only worship is illegitimate.

loved your sermon." I said, "Then you're not very smart if you loved my sermon because I'm a terrible preacher." [And he said,] "But I didn't like the worship very much." I can understand that. Now keep in mind he had just told me he had been a Christian since he was twelve years of age, and he was about thirty. And he said, "I didn't like the worship very much." [And I replied,] "I can understand that since you don't love God." He said, "What?" [And I repeated,] "I can understand that because you don't love God." Coming and making love to somebody you don't love is not much fun. You're not going to get into that, you're not going to enjoy that. That's what worship is, loving God. And if you don't love God, you're going to feel rather ridiculous in the process of trying to do it. Doing what you don't want to do just because somebody thinks you oughta do it is not much fun, is it? Everybody go like that [the congregations says,] "NOOOOOOO." It's not much fun. I just wanna make sure you're awake. And so, worshiping God when your heart's not full of love for God is a drag. My experience a year and a half ago was that it wasn't much fun. Now my problem was I knew enough about the word of God to know that if I didn't enjoy worship, there was something really wrong with me. Just like fellowship. You know, if you don't enjoy fellowship with God's people, you're in trouble, too. John, in the first [epistle of] John, he writes that, he says something to the effect that if you say you love God and you hate your brother, you don't love God. [Cf. 1 John 3.] The love of God doesn't dwell in you. If you say you love God and you can't worship him, then you don't love God at all. It just follows logically that if you love God, you'll worship him because to love God is to worship him because if you know God, you can't help but worship him.

Now I was a Christian and I thought I knew God, but I think I had gotten to a place where I didn't understand the reality of, the desire on God's part for worship. In Micah 6, he talks about—and we just read it—he talks about a very profound issue: This is all God requires of you that you do kindness and justice, and you walk humbly with your God. But to walk humbly with your God is to live the life of daily sacrifice, daily laying down your life for God, daily laying down your life in God. Today I want to illustrate these three realms of worship, these three aspects of worship—body, soul, and spirit. [I want] To take you through some Scripture. And it'll be more of a Scripture reading than teaching. I won't be able to comment too much on any of these texts because there's so many of them. I wanna give you a basis for your own exploration but keep in mind even as we start that what we're talking about is worship in three realms.

Any time you get worship into only one or two of those, you have not worshiped completely. And that is to say when we can get all three lined up, body, soul, and spirit, functioning in the same realm and working in the same way. Remember I told you one time that sometimes my body is worshiping and my spirit isn't and conversely sometimes my spirit is and my soul isn't. Now the way that would work is if you might be here physically. My body is worshiping—I'm sitting, I'm standing, I'm singing, I'm not singing, but my mind is on my car. I wonder what I'm gonna do tomorrow at work. I wonder if the roast is going to

At this point Wimber is taking a common cultural idiom and turning it on its head to define what worship is.

burn and is Aunt Sally coming over. You're in the realm of your soul—that's what your mind is. Ah, you could be a million miles away and yet sing, "Jesus loves me, this I [know] . . ." but your head, your mind is a million miles away. You've not brought your mind in correlation with your body. You've got your body here but you left your mind somewhere else. You know anything about that? Why are some of you sinking down in your seat? Set up there! You know, okay. So sometimes you mind isn't here. Bringing your mind into focus is a part of learning to worship. Now it's interesting that sometimes your spirit is worshiping and your mind and body isn't. You ever had that experience? It happens to me when I step into the shower sometimes, now don't picture that, okay, but for me when I, sometimes when I'm thinking about God, my spirit is released, and I find myself just praising the Lord, just singing to him and talking to him, you know, in my spirit. And I don't know why that's happening. It just, you know, my spirit's having a worship break, and my body and mind are somewhere else.

I was driving, driving on the freeway. I started thinking about the good things of God. My mind started worshiping. My body was driving, driving on the freeway. The next thing I know I was thinking about all the good things of God. The next thing I know, tears are running down my face. Traffic got heavy. I was coming home from LA. It was one of those two and half hour shots, you know, usually I'm fit to be tied by the time I get through there. Well, I had a great time the whole time, just driving along, worshiping God in the realm of my soul. You can get your body into worship, your mind into worship, and your spirit into worship, But the key of true worship is getting all three functioning at the same time—body, soul, and spirit.

Now let's look at some of the realms. Let's look at Psalm 95—that's a good starting point. Probably David knew more about worship than any other man who ever lived with the possible exception of Jesus. At least David wrote more by writing the Psalms about worship than any other person did. And we sense, as we read through the Psalms, you get a picture of David as a person, and we see a person who is ardently and enthusiastically and totally in love with his Creator. Even God said of David, "He's a man after my own heart. David is after having a relationship with me." [Cf. 1 Sam. 13:14.] Psalm 95, the sixth verse:

> Come, let us worship and bow down; let us kneel before the Lord our God, our maker. For he is our God, and we are the people of his pasture and the sheep of his hand. Today if you hear his voice, do not harden your hearts, as at Meribah, as in the day of Massah in the wilderness; "When your fathers tested me. . . ." [See Ps. 95:6–9a.]

Now you'll notice here physical attitudes, [some] physical activity: the activities of bowing down and kneeling down. Someone was asking me the other day about worship. And I said, "If I ever had a chance to design a sanctuary for worship, I would make sure there was a lot of space around the chairs, probably not have as many chairs as a result of it because I

In this description of David, Wimber has given the heart of his definition of what it means to worship. Notice the adverbs he uses—"ardently," "enthusiastically," and "totally."

As Wimber points out, there often is a sequence to getting the whole person involved in worship. First the body is involved, then the mind follows, and finally the spirit joins. Wimber begins his Bible exposition by looking at a Psalm verse that speaks concretely about the use of the body in different postures of worship.

think there's a great value in worship [space]." One of the things I've really enjoyed is when I was traveling a lot I worshiped in lots of different kinds of worship [spaces]." The high churches—that's not usually very popular with Protestant Evangelicals—offered a lot to me. I enjoyed the worship of the Lutherans and the Episcopalians and the Presbyterians and the Catholics. I liked the physical involvement that was required to worship in their churches. They drew me into doing it. It wouldn't have been enough for my personal taste to have ended there, but I liked the taste I got in it. It was a nice place to visit, but I wouldn't want to live there. I enjoyed that; I just didn't like the formality of it. You know, I didn't want to dress all up to go do it. But I did like the doing of it. I did like the kneeling and the bowing. It was very, very helpful to get my body going so that it could get my mind going. . . . The body's the first issue usually. If I get my body down to worship, I can get my mind down to it, and then my spirit is released. Do you know anything about that?

Psalm 66—that's back to the left for those of you who know your left from your right—66:4, let's read from 1 to 4:

> Shout joyfully to God, all the earth; Sing the glory of his name; Make his praise glorious. Say to God, "How awesome are thy works! Because of the greatness of thy power thine enemies will give feigned obedience to thee. All the earth will worship thee, [and will] sing praises to thee; [They will] sing praises to thy name."

Boy, David really knew how to get it on, didn't he? Shout joyfully, all the earth. Can you picture that? Can you picture the whole earth shouting joyfully? That's going to happen, you know? That's what it's talking about in Romans in [the] eighth chapter, the ninth chapter, it's the sixth chapter when it talks about all the creation groans in travail waiting for the Creator.[2] When the creator comes, all the creation's gonna flip out in praise to God. I can't wait to hear that happen. And remember another occasion when Jesus was coming in the east gate into Jerusalem. And they said, "Hey, you gonna let these guys ah, you know, worship you in this way?" [And Jesus replied,] "If I didn't, these stones would cry out." [Cf. Luke 19:40.] I didn't know the stones could do that. I suspect they could if he said that. So, "all of the creation will shout unto the Lord," [will] sing unto the Lord, give praise unto the Lord, for who he is and what he has done for us.

Look at Psalm 100:

> Shout joyfully to the Lord, all the earth. Serve the Lord with gladness. . . . Know that the Lord himself is God; It is he who made us and not we ourselves; For we are his people and the sheep of his pasture. Enter his gates with thanksgiving, and his courts with praise. Give thanks to

Before his involvement with this congregation, Wimber traveled extensively in the mid-1970s as a Church Growth consultant with Fuller Theological Seminary. This position brought him into contact with churches across a variety of denominations.

---

2. Wimber probably means Romans 8:22.

him; bless his name. For the Lord is good; His loving kindness is everlasting, and his faithfulness to all generations. [Ps.100:1–5]

Now here is a transition from the active of shouting and praising and serving and coming before the Lord—all in a physical domain—to the inner reality of what's prompting it, which is the knowledge of who God is. Look at the third verse. Know that the Lord himself is God. That is to say, have experience, know this, acknowledge this, think on this, get your mind thinking on who the Lord is. Know the Lord himself is God. He's our creator. We didn't make ourselves. He created us. We are his people, and the sheep of his pasture.

Wimber is following the sequence he suggested earlier: The body worships first, and the mind follows.

Notice the attitude expressed in the next verse: Enter his gates with thanksgiving. You see, it's a natural thing, when you start thinking of what God is, who he is, what he's done for you. The natural response to that is thankfulness: "Gee, hey, you're great."

I remember one time hearing a sermon on worship. And I thought, "Well, does God want us to butter him up? Is that what he's looking for?" You see, I misunderstood a very elemental thing about all the works of God and that is that they're not for him, they're for me. God is teaching me to worship for my benefit.

I can remember when I was a kid, going to the Grand Canyon. We came out from Illinois, and we came out to the Grand Canyon and we just stood there. And the natural thing you do is—do what? [Wimber responds to something said to him at this moment from the congregation.] Ha, ha. Benny, take him home, will you? Some of us who have more couth would say, "oh and ah!" and be moved by the "ah" [grandeur]. We wouldn't try to fill it otherwise. We'd be moved by the grandeur of it all and how big it is, and, in our spiritual realm, [we] respond. . . .

And so the beginning of worship in our soul is to acknowledge who God is. Just to know it. Jesus talked about this on several occasions. Remember that in the New Testament we have a Greek word meaning experiential knowledge, knowledge gained by experience. In John the fourth chapter, [it reads:] "We worship that which we do know. You worship that which you don't know. You worship that which you've only heard about [but] we worship that which we've experienced."[3] So when you've experienced God, to experience him is to be able to worship him.

In fact, there's a relationship between the rate and the amount and the quality of the experience you're having with God and how easy it is to worship. And I've found in my own life that worship is becoming a characteristic of my daily living. [It is] Not only worship in a sense of responding to God in emotion but in the area of ethics and values and all that I'm feeling. I want to reflect the presence of God in all that I do.

Let's look at Psalm 103, one of the really precious psalms. Read the first four verses: "Bless the Lord, O my soul, and all that is within me, bless his holy name" [Ps. 103:1]. The

---

3. Wimber is paraphrasing Jesus's discussion with the Samaritan woman at the well in John 4:22.

soul and the mind are the same realm. "Bless the Lord with your mind" means to think on the Lord, reflect [on] the Lord. Sort through all the things you know about God. Have you ever done that? Have you ever just started sorting through and said, "Lord, I praise you for being the creator of the world, and the universe and of me and of puppies" and just, you know, go through his acts of creation?

Thank you for the sun and the moon and the stars. I like you for, I thank you for beaches and for mountains and things and Crackerjacks and whatever it is that you like him for—that he created. He didn't create Crackerjacks. I don't think he did, anyway.

And then talk about, you know, like he's the alpha and the omega, the beginning and the end. [See Rev. 21:6.] You know, Jesus is the bookends to time. He started it, and he'll end it. That's very comforting to me. To know that, no matter how long it is, I'm going to end up with him just as I started with him. There's a security in that. Just begin praising God for the things he has done for you, for the life he's [given you]. . . .You don't own the next breath you take. He does. You don't own the whole heartbeat that you have. He can stop that whole system. You don't own anything. You're owned by him. Just begin thanking him for those things. Bless the Lord, O my soul, and all that is within me, bless his holy name.

"Bless the Lord, O my soul, and forget none of his benefits."[4] Review the benefits, go through the benefits. The things you've accrued are dividends of the relationship you have with God. He "pardons all of your iniquities." Do you know what a pardon is? That's better than being forgiven. A pardon is to wipe it out. Yes, you're guilty, but yes, you're forgiven. I pardon you. Iniquities means "lawlessness." [The Lord] wipes out your lawlessness. Don't you like that? I like that. [He] wipes out your lawlessness. [The Lord] "heals all of your diseases." How many does that include? All of your diseases. He "redeems your life from the pit." Remember the pit? Yeah, you do. He "crowns you with love and compassion; [he] satisfies your years with good things."

I remember one time talking to a guy, and he was a Christian and I wasn't. He had been a Christian about 20 years. [And I said,] "Anybody'd be a Christian the way you've [i.e., the guy] got it made. You've got a beautiful home. You've got a lovely family. Money in the bank. You got a good job." [And he replied,] "But I became a Christian when I didn't have these things. The reason I have them is because the Lord has satisfied my years with good things." He quoted the scripture to me. [See Ps. 103:5.] You see, it's a dividend of the Christian life to have things. Not things to have you, [but] you to have things. It's part of the package. God wants to bless you. If you don't have things, it's probably because you haven't let him bless. Get in the swing of it, man.

"Satisfies your years with good things so that your youth is renewed like an eagle." And it

Wimber's quick wit sometimes seemed to work by stream of consciousness, like the reference to Crackerjacks here. And yet in the next few sentences he comes back to the most profound issues.

---

4. Psalm 103:2. As he proceeds to lists the "benefits," Wimber is citing from verses 3 and following in this psalm.

goes on and on and on. One of the aspects of worship is to review in the realm of your mind the things that God has done. The things that God has done generally and specifically for you.

Let's look into the New Testament: John 4. We have worship then in the realm of our bodies, the things we do, the activities of worship. We have worship then in the realms of our mind. The things we think. Now we're going to deal with the realms of our spirit. You remember the occasion is that Jesus is talking to a woman at the well. They have been discussing religion. And in the 22nd verse of the fourth chapter of John, [we find]: "You worship that which you do not know. We worship that which we know, for salvation is from the Jews." Remember he was talking to a lady who was only partially Jewish. She was Syrian and Jewish, Syrian and Israeli. [And it continues in the] 23rd verse: "But an hour is coming and it now is when the true worshipers shall worship the Father in spirit and truth." The hour is coming and still is. That is to say, the hour is now come, lady, when we're not going to worship geographically. She had just pointed to a mountain and said, "Our fathers told us to worship up there. Your fathers said to worship down in Jerusalem." [And Jesus replied,] "The hour is now come in which you're going to worship in spirit and truth, for such people the Father seeks to be his worshipers."[5] The Father has sent the Son to find those who will worship the Father in spirit and truth.

Here's the reason why [in] the twenty-fourth verse: "Because God is spirit." You wanna talk to God, talk to him spirit to spirit. Why? Because God is spirit. "God is spirit, and those who worship him must worship him in spirit and in truth," meaning in spirit and in reality. How do you go about worshiping God in your spirit? Well, there's a lot in the Word on this subject. Let's look at Philippians 3:3 for a moment. Keep in mind that you can worship God in the realm of your body. You can worship God in the realm of your soul. And many of us have never known worship in any other way, we've been worshiping, that worship we have done has been in our bodies and in our souls. But the New Testament calls for a new reality of worship, which is the worship from spirit to spirit.

Philippians 3:3. Let me read 3, [actually] 1 through 3 because it'll make more sense. Keep in mind Paul usually divides his letters up with doctrine and application. Here's the application of some doctrine. He's done some teaching. He loves the Philippians. It's a very, very happy letter. Here in the third chapter, first verse, he says, "Finally, brethren. Rejoice in the Lord. To write the same things again is no trouble to me and is a safeguard to you. Beware of the dogs, beware of the evil workers, beware of the false circumcision." He's already warned them about these people and he's saying look out for them. "For we are the true circumcision" [Phil. 3:3]. Now he's saying that—keep in mind that the Jews were circumcised physically to represent an internal work of the heart. He says we are the true circumcision. The

---

5. Wimber is paraphrasing John 4:23.

word "heart" means "spirit." [They are] The same realm. The heart and the spirit are one and the same thing.

"For we are the true circumcision." We are the true worshipers who worship in the spirit of God. That is to say, when your spirit is revitalized through being born again, when your spirit is filled, ah, ah, when you have a fullness of the Spirit ah, through ensuing works of grace in your life. Then you have a greater capacity to worship spirit to spirit. Now, you have no capacity to worship spirit to spirit before you are born again. You can't do it. You can't worship God because your spirit is dead. Dead spirits don't worship. It has to become alive to worship. So, here in this verse we have the understanding that we are the true circumcision, we are the true people of God who have learned to worship God in spirit.

Look with me to Colossians the third chapter. Now we have a strain of thinking that's in Ephesians 5, Colossians 3, and 1 Corinthians 14 that teaches the premise of worship concerning this business of when we gather together we are to do certain activities. We see that articulated here in the third chapter, the sixteenth verse. It says, "Let the word of Christ richly dwell in you, with all wisdom, teaching and admonishing one another with psalms, hymns and spiritual songs." Now I taught this a few weeks ago but for those of you who weren't here "psalms" means the Psalms, and the Greek word *psalmos* means to review the Psalms. So when we come together, what do we do? We sing a few songs, and Bob will read a psalm. Quite often, we'll do it back and forth, but the idea is to refresh ourselves out of the Psalms. The Psalms were given for praise. The Psalms were given for equipping us and ushering into the presence of God. [And] So we come together to recite the psalms and in some cases sing them. We sang Psalm 5 in the first service today. Every now and then we sing a psalm. That's hard to say.

Then we have hymns. Hymns means canticles, popular odes, popular melodies. And we sang several of those in this service. These are the contemporary songs about Jesus. We sang, the last song we sang, was "Jesus, Jesus." What was the last one in this one? He added another one. Oh yeah, "Jesus, I just wanna thank you."[6] That would come under this heading of hymns, and the Greek word is canticles.

And then [there are] spiritual songs. Now [about] spiritual songs, if you take the three texts in the New Testament [that use the phrase], it can mean nothing other than singing in the spirit. That's when your spirit is singing in what the New Testament calls tongues. Now spiritual songs are the release of your spirit where God is speaking through you and to himself. And let's turn to 1 Corinthians 14, and you can see how the dynamic of that works. Don't get hung up on the form of how you do it at this point. Let's just deal with the theology of it.

In the sequence of worshiping God through our bodies, through our minds (souls), and through our spirits (hearts), the last has a special place because it is the one we cannot do in our own abilities. Wimber seems to be saying that God must renew a human spirit by a new birth before a person can worship God in that dimension.

Wimber's statement about being "ushered into the presence of God" anticipates what will become a popular, late 20th-century way of speaking. This phrase and similar ones (e.g., "enter into worship" or "enter into God's presence") speak about what happens symbolically or inwardly in worship.

Wimber is poking fun at himself. He means that he has a hard time saying "sing a psalm" because of the alliteration with the letter "s."

6. Perhaps Wimber is referring to two songs written by Bill and Gloria Gaither earlier in the 1970s: "There's Something about That Name" (copyright 1970 William J. Gaither, Inc. Admin. by Gaither Copyright Management) and "Jesus, We Just Want to Thank You" (copyright 1974 by William J. Gaither, Inc. Admin. by Gaither Copyright Management).

Somebody moved Corinthians. Ah, here it is. 1 Corinthians 14:2, I think, is where I want to go. Yeah, 14:2. It's not a horizontal but a vertical [dimension when one speaks in tongues]. 14:2 [reads], "For one who speaks in tongues does not speak to men." Now notice that relationship. When you're speaking in tongues or singing in tongues [that is,] spiritual songs, you're speaking to God, not to men. [It is] Not a horizontal but a vertical [dimension in worship]. "No one understands but in his spirit he speaks mysteries." [See 1 Cor. 14:2b.]

The person speaking in tongues can't understand it any more than the person hearing it unless there's a supernatural gift involved, which is the gift of interpretation.

On very rare occasions, one, three, or four occasions in our church we've had somebody speak in tongues, and we've had an interpretation. I think on two or three of those occasions I've had the interpretation.

Somebody asked me one time what is that like. It's like reciting something without your mind in gear. When you have an interpretation in a public meeting, you're not thinking of it at all. You could no more not say that than anything. It bubbles out from inside of you. It comes out. It's almost automatic. It's almost ah, there's almost no control over it. For me, I don't even know what I'm saying. I don't know the sentence structure or the words. They come out and, when it's over, I ask somebody what am I saying. I somehow can't hear it very well. I get so turned on I can't hear it. I can't think.

But that's an automatic thing. That's God causing through his Spirit a person speaking a language they don't know and another person on the other end to interpret the language that they don't know through, not even through their mind, just spirit to spirit.

"No one understands for in his spirit he speaks mysteries. But one who prophesies. . . ." If you want to build the body up, you don't do it through speaking in tongues. You build the body up through prophesying, and that is again a supernatural manifestation of God under the authority and the anointing of God. Prophesying is something that, ah, the best I can describe it is sort of like I used to have a car years ago that had a thing called overdrive. And you're driving along and there's a certain amount of friction. You put it in overdrive, and it's kind of like gliding. In fact, they used to have a little car called power drive that did that. Tells you how old I am. The friction's reduced. Sometimes when I'm teaching I could take you back on some of the tapes that I've got for the year and a half of preaching. I can show you where I've stopped preaching and began prophesying. It just switched gears. I was not thinking any longer. Just witnessing to what God was doing. Moving from one realm—the realm of my mind—inspired, I'm turned on by a thing that God has taught so I'm teaching it. It's [i.e., his prophesying] not the same level as Scripture God [is] speaking through his servant.

Notice in the fourth verse he comes back to the issue of tongues: "One who speaks in tongues edifies himself." There's a benefit even if you don't understand. That's why we pray in our closets and alone. And we speak in tongues without any interpretation. What kind of stroke is that? What do you get out of that? All I know is that, ah, it feels good. After it's

Wimber launches into an extended discussion of the nature and proper biblical use of glossolalia (speaking or singing in tongues) in worship. Remember that he was expounding on worshiping through the body, then the mind, and, finally, the spirit. That latter point had brought him to a passage that spoke about "spiritual songs," which he interprets as singing in tongues. Referring to tongues in that instance triggers this extended time of careful explanation of tongues in worship. Wimber is not insisting that speaking or singing in tongues is the only way to worship God "in spirit."

Wimber addresses a natural question in Charismatic churches: If prophesying (and interpretation of tongues) is speech given directly by God, does it have the same authority as Scripture? His answer is no.

done, quite after, I feel a great sense of God's presence and a strong feeling of elation, of joy, of God having ministered to me. I'm gonna keep doing it until it feels bad. One who speaks in a tongue edifies himself so if you're praying for some kind of spiritual gift in the church [remember that] prophecy is a much more functional gift. One who speaks in a tongue edifies himself, [but] one who speaks in prophecy edifies the church. That's why we make a basic—I don't know if we've ever made a stand—we emphasize teaching in the mind.

Every now and then a Pentecostal brother will come visit and say, "Your church doesn't get it on. You don't do enough this or that." God bless you. There's lots of churches that do that. But we're really doing what we feel is a scriptural balance. The emphases of worship are the realm of the mind, releasing the spirit. But the emphases of worship are the realm of the mind. That's what God is after.

Let's look at the fifth verse again for a moment, the fourth verse, the third verse—excuse me, I turned too far, the fourth verse: "One who speaks in a tongue edifies himself, [but] one who prophesies edifies the church. Now I wish that you all spoke in tongues but even more that you [would] prophesy." Paul says "Hey, this is a better deal." Prophesying has more value in a public setting. Greater is the one who prophesies than the one who speaks in tongues unless he interprets so that the church may receive. "Now brethren, if I came to you speaking in tongues, what should I profit you [unless I speak to you] either by revelation or knowledge or prophecy or teaching?"[7]

Now those are three gifts. And yet even lifeless things—he talks about instruments and how they function—if they just play to a bunch of sound, there's no melody [cf. 1 Cor. 13:1], but you've got to pick individual notes that are played on the flute of the heart. For if the bugle produces an indistinct sound, who will prepare himself for battle? How will it be known what is spoken, for you will be speaking into the air. There are perhaps a great many kinds of languages in the world. No kinds without meaning. If I do not know the meaning of the language, I shall be as one who speaks as a barbarian and the one who speaks will be a barbarian to me. "So also since you are zealous of spiritual gifts then seek to abound for the edification of the church" [1 Cor. 14:12]. That is to say, the preponderance of scripture is for the edification of the church. Edification of the church is the issue, not self-edification. Therefore, tongues is subordinate. Ministering in the realm of our mind is the dominant factor. Prophecy is the dominant factor.

I feel very strongly that we worship in a very theologically sound framework. Somebody said, "Well, you forbid to speak in tongues." [My answer is,] "No, [we don't.]" Not self-edification when you come together to worship. Edification of the church is the issue, not self-edification. Prophesying is the dominant factor. I think the Scripture is very strong on the issue. Frankly, on one or two occasions, someone has spoken in tongues while there

---

7. 1 Corinthians 14:6. The apostle Paul is speaking about the most useful of his own speaking ministries.

An important distinction often found in tongue-speaking churches is the one between public and private use of tongues. Wimber notes that private, devotional speaking in tongues has benefits (in the "prayer closet"), but the main emphasis of his teaching here is its proper role in public worship.

Wimber returns to his original goal of advocating a whole-person worship of the Lord. In his approach, worshiping in spirit (i.e., with speaking in tongues) should not be divorced from worshiping with one's mind. Thus, prophecy which calls to mind who the Lord is and what the Lord has done is critical. Wimber is trying to make a case against those who suggest that the Vineyard congregation did not speak in tongues often enough in corporate worship.

was already a ministry of the Lord going on. That interruption is not typical in the Lord at all. And so, I've had to go and admonish and say, "Bless you sister, bless you brother, but this is what the Lord says on this subject: Order is the issue of scripture; order is the issue of worship."

[Consider 1 Corinthians 14, the] 40th verse: "But let all things be done properly and in an orderly manner." The admonishment of scripture again and again is for balance and order [as in] 1 Corinthians 14:40.

Let's go back to the 13th verse one more time: "Therefore, let one who speaks in a tongue pray that he may interpret." If you are having an experience of worship, you sense that God wants you to speak in tongues, pray for interpretation, make sure you're in a proper position for speaking in tongues. If you're a new person in the body [of Christ], you'll probably be asked not to do it because we don't know you. We don't know what your background is. We don't know where you're coming from. The scripture is very strong about recognizing those who lead. If you've been in the body, and you're certain the Holy Spirit is prompting you to do it, then get it on. And we'll pray, and God will give us an interpretation. If he doesn't give us an interpretation, you were probably responding to a carnal impulse.

I was in a meeting one time in Tennessee. There were about 4,000 people there. Suddenly, right in the middle of somebody's sermon, someone else gave a tongue. They spoke for several minutes, and then there was dead silence afterwards. I waited, and I waited—along with all those thousands of people—and no one had an interpretation.

After the meeting was over, I went to the leader of the meeting, leader of the group of pastors. [I asked,] "What happened there?" [He replied,] "Well, what happened was that a brother that spoke in tongues wasn't prompted by the Holy Spirit." [I asked again,] "What do you mean? You mean that was the devil?" [He answered,] "No." "How do you know that?" "There was no interpretation."

God will not honor that in a meeting, and so, from time to time, in your own enthusiasm you can step out in a realm and God won't honor it. You have to be really sensitive to the use of gifts—that it's really the Lord. On the other hand, if the Lord's encouraging you to do, and you're not doing it, you're quenching the Spirit, that it's really the Lord encouraging you to do it. You have to be very sensitive between the two. You see what's happening. When your mind is in gear, you're praying in one realm. When your spirit is in gear, you're praying in another realm. Never the twain shall meet.

[1 Corinthians 14, the] Fifteenth verse: "What is the outcome then? I will pray with the spirit, and I will pray with the mind also. I will sing with the spirit, and I will sing with the mind also. Otherwise, if you bless in the spirit only, how will the one who fills the place of the ungifted say 'Amen' [at your giving of thanks, since he does not know what you are saying]?"

This is a funny thing too that somebody asked me the other day: "Can I be a member of your body?" [I answered,] "Well, since we don't have members, I guess you can be." [The

With this example Wimber makes clear that a public speaking in tongues should be followed by an interpretation also given by the Holy Spirit for the edification of the whole body. Ecstatic speech is not an end to itself in corporate worship.

person asked,] "Do I have to speak in tongues to be a member of your fellowship?" "Oh no," I said. I hope we never gather around the issue of speaking in tongues. That's peripheral, that's secondary. We gather because we love Jesus. If you love Jesus, you're welcome. If you're committed to the Word of God, you're welcome.

Praise the Lord. That's what we're here for—to praise the Lord, to bless Jesus. I would really be hung up if I thought there was anybody [that] thought they had to go through some gymnastics whether it be valid scripturally or not in order to be partakers in the group. Our fellowship is not around the gifts of the Spirit. Our fellowship is around the giver of the Spirit, Jesus Christ himself. Somebody say "Amen" or blink or something. Do you believe that? Alright.

What the scripture is admonishing here is that "All things be done decently and in order" [1 Cor. 14:40]. Somebody who comes into the group and doesn't have those particular gifts won't be offended and turned off and put off. What were they doing over there? What was that that was going on there? Was that the Lord?

I remember the first time I had an experience of going to a camp meeting in the South. This was about three years ago. Our plane was late getting into Memphis, Tennessee. So I finally got off the plane at seven o'clock and got in an old truck, and we [went] out to the hills of Tennessee. If you haven't been in the south in the summer, you don't know what hot is. [This] camp meeting [had] maybe six or seven thousand people in [it]. It was about nine o'clock when we got there. The meeting had been going on since two o'clock in the afternoon. They sang until eleven o'clock that night. When they finally quit singing, I mentioned to the guy I was sitting next to, "Boy, that's a long song service, two hours." He said, "We've been singing since two o'clock in the afternoon." They'd been singing for nine hours straight at those meetings. If you think our services are long, you gotta go to a down south camp service. They have a beautiful time in the Lord. And it's very culturally right on.

Many of you would be extremely uncomfortable worshiping in that kinda setting. It would just blow your mind. They do some pretty wild things. It's right for them. God bless them. He visits their sanctuary. The Lord responds to their needs. We don't have to do it the way they do it, but we have to do it. Worship is a prerequisite for the Christian life. It's the foundation of the Christian life. Worship God in everything you do and say. Worship him in all deeds, worship him in all thoughts. [Worship him] In the sanctuary of your inner being. Worship him through the spirit, worship him in your body. [Worship him] with your finances. Worship him with your relationships at home. Worship him on the freeway. Lock, stock, and barrel. No holds barred. Everything you have. All you ever hoped to be lay at his feet.

Father, we praise you. We thank you for teaching us to worship, for giving us a heart full of love for you, [and] for helping us be unashamed of the affection, the love we have for you. O God, fill our hearts that we might worship you throughout the week [with the] affection and love we feel for you in every realm of our lives, that we would keep you ever present, that you

This opinion was one of the common dividing lines between classical Pentecostalism, which usually insisted on speaking in tongues as a sign of being "baptized in the Spirit," and the Charismatic Renewal Movement, which accepted the use of tongues without insisting on it.

Wimber returns to his main point: The appropriate worship of God involves the whole human person in all of that person's life. His concluding prayer mentions a critical part of his own journey in worship (and surely it was the same for many of the Vineyard worshipers)—learning to be unashamed and comfortable with the intense, authentic expressions of affection which characterize this approach to worship.

would be in the back of our minds throughout the day, singing in our spirits, that you would help us, Lord, moment to moment to be constantly practicing your presence that we might be a people of worship and praise and therefore be a light. . . .

Source: John Wimber, "Loving God," in *The Ministry and Teachings of John Wimber* series, CD #303 (Doin' the Stuff/Vineyard Music Group, 2004). Used by permission: Sean and Christy Wimber, 2015 @ Yorba Linda Vineyard/Wimber. Global.

## Excerpts from "Why Do We Worship?"

*Desiring to lay out solid scriptural and theological foundations for his church's worship, Wimber explores the inevitability of worship and thus the need to worship the God revealed in Jesus Christ in the following sermon excerpts. Worship as lifestyle and God's gracious response to true love expressed for him are themes that also emerge in this sermon.*

. . . We have been commanded, we have been chosen, and we have been created to worship. And here's where we get ourselves into the biggest mess because, since we're created to worship, if we don't know God, we'll worship gods of our own making. We'll worship the nearest god, we'll worship the local god, we'll worship the first one presented to us. We'll worship the first thing that comes our way, we'll worship the first thing the enemy provides along the way, because we will worship. Everybody's a worshiper. I pointed that out to the man I was sitting next to in the plane because, after about 5 hours I was getting to the point where I thought, "I can't get through to this guy." And so at one point in time I said, "You know you're created to worship." He said, "What do you mean?" And I said, "Well, your very nature, your very makeup, is, the Bible tells us, is that [you are] created to worship. You're worshiping now." And he said, "What do you mean, I'm 'worshiping now'?" And I said, "Well, you've been telling me about all the things you've done, and the money you've made, and the position you have and how your company is advancing, and it is advancing at other times when your competitors are declining, and that it's largely to your own initiative and to your own genius and your ability to get things done." I said, "You've been worshiping for several hours. You've been talking about yourself the whole time. You are your god." (I get nasty when I don't win, you see, right?) I said, "You are your god." I said, "You've been telling me," and I said, "I lost count, I think you've said it somewhere like 75 times that you don't need God." I said, "The reason you don't need God is you have got a god, and you're it." And he grinned . . . and he was just staring at me. And I knew I made a point at this one. And I said, "Frankly, I don't want to join you in your worship." And I know this was the only revelatory thing I got the whole time. I had been praying my prayer, you know, the one I had told you about, "OH GOD!"—that one, you know, like that. I had been praying the whole time for 5 hours. Nothing

Wimber is referring to a story he had told earlier in the sermon. In this story Wimber's heart to evangelize is apparent.

had happened. Finally, at this one point, I said, "I know there was a time in your life you cried out to God." And right at that point a little moisture came to his eyes, and he said, "When I was six I asked God, 'If you're really real, show me.'" I said, "Well, what I want you to know is that God heard that prayer, and the process is on right now, buddy, and he's gonna show you." And then he dismissed that immediately like, "Well, you Christians, you always say those kinds of things." He says, "You want to make me afraid." And so then we talked at great length about why would Christians want to make somebody afraid? Why would we say things that would frighten them? He says, "You talk about hell, and you talk about this or that. When I die, there'll be nothing." I said, "Good luck." I said, "You will have done good if there's nothing. Oblivion." But I said, "It's not gonna be that way." I said, "And if *you're* right, then there *will* be oblivion. If I'm right, you're in *big* trouble." So we did get down to it at a couple points there. You see, we are created to worship and we'll worship something of our own hands. . . .

. . . You see, we'll either make something of our own hands, or we'll go to the Creator who made us. See, the only reason that we can make something is because we've been created, and we've been created for a purpose, and that purpose is to give ourselves in worship to God. And, as I said, there's the direct application as we assemble together as the body of Christ and worship the Lord, but then there's the indirect as we move out of this building and worship the Lord all week long in the way we spend our money and in the way we drive our cars, and the way that we treat our children and our husbands and wives, and in the way that we show respect for our neighbors and relate to the people around us. You see, there's a worship of God in all that because you have a constant awareness of God's presence and work in all that you're doing, and so it's not some sort of compartmentalized Christianity where you're just worshiping God, you know, an hour or two a week. And I'm afraid that in some cases, some of us are sort of hour-or-two-a-week Christians. We really don't see ourselves as taking Christ to work with us. And/or relating to him in every kind of context, in every kind of setting. The way we pay our bills, the way we sell our used cars, you know, there's real Christianity when you can take Jesus into the way you deal business-wise with people, where you really want to give the other person a good deal because you want to honor them as someone that God would honor. That you could bless them in a way that would evidence that Christ indeed is in control of your finances and still trust Christ that somehow, though you may not get the better of the other person in the transaction, that he will still meet your needs, in fact, more than meet your needs, give you the ability to meet other people's needs. All of this is with a conscious awareness that you have been created. Commanded, chosen, and created to worship God. . . .

. . . But you see, somewhere, someplace, there's gotta be a people that will worship God, that will *give* themselves to it, and I make no apologies in the Vineyard that throughout the Vineyard and worldwide, wherever the Vineyard is, that our number one priority is worship. And by that I do not mean just the activity of singing the lovely songs that God has given us to sing, which do express our heart and are an index of our commitment to Christ, but it

To understand the impact of Wimber's teaching, one should remember how overwhelming the corporate worship experiences could be. It would have been easy to be attracted to the weekly worship service, enjoy it, and then live one's life out of a different approach to God. But Wimber is insistent: All of life—inside and outside of a worship service—should be worship to God. Why is it so easy to separate worship in a service and worship as a way of life?

*starts* with the expression of love to God in worship. And [let's go] clear back now to where I started. Some of you are brand new with us, and you might wonder what in the world we're doing here, you know, the first half hour or so. What we're doing is, by the songs that we sing, trying to express in contemporary idioms and in intimate language, the love that we feel for God. And we believe that, as we do so, that God is touched by that, and that he will respond and confer on us his presence because of that love-making that goes on with the expressing of our intimate care for God. And over the years we've experienced his presence when we do that. We've experienced his favor when we do that. And that's *all* kind of like a vortex through which we see our Christianity: that otherwise, what we do in that half hour oughta characterize our whole week. We should constantly be singing these songs, constantly reviewing our care and our love for our God. And in every transaction, and in every exchange, whether it's the water cooler or finding a parking spot, we need to learn how to honor our God in the way we defer to and care for people. You got it? And that's Christianity.

Wimber concisely describes the theological dynamic he sees in the extended time of music that begins a service. This description explains his understanding of what happens in worship. Having hearts moved is critical, both on our part and on God's part. Wimber states that God is touched by the church's honest expression of intimate love toward him and, consequently, blesses the worshiping assembly with his divine presence.

---

Source: John Wimber, "Why Do We Worship?," in *The Ministry and Teachings of John Wimber* series, CD #9892 (Doin' the Stuff/Vineyard Music Group, 2004). Used by permission: Sean and Christy Wimber, 2015 @ Yorba Linda Vineyard/Wimber. Global.

## *Excerpts from "Don't Lose Your First Love"*

*The following excerpts come from a sermon John Wimber preached at the end of 1978 or beginning of 1979, based on dating within it. This material is direct from the early years, not yet summarized or domesticated by later historical reflection. Here Wimber connects the origins of his Vineyard congregation to the broader movement of "new style" churches in Southern California and elsewhere. Tongue in cheek, he even gives a "formula" for starting one of these new churches: mix a Bible, a teacher, and a rock band. Wimber also notes his congregation's ministry responsibility in the larger phenomenon. Liturgically, Wimber discusses the congregation's practice of infant dedication and what he understands it to mean. The final excerpt calls the congregation back to the intensity of love for God it had in its first days, based on a text from Revelation.*

Wimber refers to Chuck Smith, pastor of the Calvary Chapel congregation in Costa Mesa, California, a short distance south of Anaheim. Smith's ministry to hippies in the late 1960s and early 1970s made his church a prominent leader in the Jesus People movement. Wimber's congregation was originally associated with the Calvary Chapel churches and was known as the Calvary Chapel of Yorba Linda.

. . . Now in our times, we've had a very similar experience in Costa Mesa. And as a result of the hippie movement a number of years ago God reached out through several people, Chuck Smith being one of them, and began ministering to the kids that were going up and down the coast highway in those days and began communicating to them in such a way that they became Christians. And as a result the best we know more than a hundred thousand people have been converted in the last nearly ten years as a result of that movement. And the result of *that* is that there are churches all over the western United States, and a few in the eastern, and a few in Europe now, and in the Philippines, and a few in the far East that have come directly from that ministry, and this church is one of those that has been influenced by and is a part of the rippling effect of the movement of God. . . .

. . . And it was much the same way as our churches have been started. Most of the pastors, we have over a hundred Calvary chapels now in the Southern California area up to Northern California, a few in Oregon, a few in other states, but there's over a hundred now. Just, just in the last year, since May of '78 (which is only, what, 8 months? 7 months. 8 months. 7 months. Ah, 8, counting this one) there have been over 60 new ones started. These churches are spawning very rapidly, and one of the reasons that they're spawning very rapidly is that they're started almost exclusively by laymen, that is to say people with a minimal Bible education who have just been converted in the church and as a result they feel led to go out, and they usually start a Bible study or work some place, and the next thing you know they have a church of four or five hundred or a thousand, or, or whatever. It's called "insta-church." All you have to do is take a Bible, a teacher, and a rock band, and you put them together, and you mix them, and, you know, there's nothing to it. And the result is that there are all of these baby, these fledgling churches that need encouragement and help, and, as we shared last week, we shared with a new one that was just starting, and we gave some of our resources to them and will continue to encourage them and look after them, and try to, you know, help them get underway. And God has given us that kind of ministry with several of them.

. . . And I think it's important to recognize that God doesn't have any grandchildren, that every generation must be won to Christ in and of itself, that we can't expect even our children, being raised in, in our Christian training hour, in hearing you pray and watching you witness, and maybe you, watching your lives, you can't expect them to grow up and just assume that they're gonna become Christians. It's a battle from the day they're born to win them to Christ. And everything in our society, everything, it seems everything in our society and most everything that they come in contact with will contaminate and work to draw them away from that relationship with Christ that you will, that they'll have. Every now and then when we have a baby dedication, the, the enormity of what we're doing there really strikes me, when we lay hands on parents, and we say, "God, bless this family. They intend, [and] they commit themselves to raising these children in your nurture." And what they're doing is declaring war on one who has declared war on them, and from that day forward, the enemy will try, if he can, to snatch those kids away from them, and away from the God that they intended to dedicate them to.

. . . And he [i.e., Christ] says this to the church of Ephesus, and he begins with this first point. He says, "Remember, therefore, from where you have fallen" [Rev. 2:5]. When I talked about the bread of life[8] a couple weeks ago, this text was in my mind. We had been studying it on Wednesday mornings, and the Lord had stirred it to my remembrance, and I remember

The Anaheim Vineyard congregation did not practice infant baptism but did practice baby dedication, a service in which parents offered up their children to the Lord and the church requested God's blessing upon that household.

---

8. Perhaps a reference to Jesus's teaching about himself as the bread of life in John 6.

By April 1977, the original group had grown to about 100 persons.

After moving from a home setting, the congregation met in a Masonic Lodge building from May 1977 through July 1977.

"Baptized in the Spirit" is a technical term used in the Charismatic Movement and Pentecostalism for a second, defining infilling of the Holy Spirit. The term is biblical, drawn from Acts, an important book in Charismatic and Pentecostal spirituality.

that when this fellowship started, ah, just a year and a half ago, that, there, some of us who were here then, and, and many of you weren't, but some of us that were here then had an expectation. I'm telling you, some of you would have worked in the nursery for Jesus you were so ardent, you know? Huh? You would've done *anything*, and you often volunteered to. I can remember the first few weeks that we gathered, I mean, we would gather an hour and a half before the church service. People would start coming in. Remember at the old Masonic Lodge? And you would move furniture and take care, some of you, you know, took care of babies that never take care of babies. Some of you, you know, taught that never teach. Some of you became Sunday School teachers in that time and, you know, haven't done it since. And some of you, you know, I mean, you know what I mean? You would've done *anything* for Jesus. Why? Because you were so excited, so turned on. I can remember scenes of people embracing and weeping and praying over each other. It was so precious and beautiful, and every time the Lord would add to the Body [of Christ]—remember?—every time the Lord would add someone new to the Body, I mean, we would just, it was so intimate and so close and then something started happening. Sorta became commonplace, you know? And, I don't know about you, you may not even have noticed it, but last week, I think, I don't know the exact number, Mark kinda takes care of this, but I think there were over 20 people that came forward last week to be baptized in the Spirit and, a few that were healed, and one or two that were saved. You know, and, we say, "Oh, ha ha, that's what we do almost every week," you know, it's like, you know? But there, there was a time when we had an appetite for those things that, I mean, we couldn't *wait* for Sunday. I can remember all day Saturday getting phone calls all day long. [People would ask,] "Is it, is it soup yet? No? Can't we have a little meeting for tomorrow, you know, just to get us by, you know, for the day? Ha, just a little something for the road?" Remember those days? Jesus says to the church in Ephesus, he says: "Remember, therefore, from where you've fallen." Remember where you were, Ephesians? Remember when that, that love affair was too hot to cool down?

---

Source: John Wimber, "Don't Lose Your First Love," in *The Ministry and Teachings of John Wimber* series, CD #310 (Doin' the Stuff/Vineyard Music Group, 2004). Used by permission: Sean and Christy Wimber, 2015 @ Yorba Linda Vineyard/Wimber. Global.

## Excerpts from "Essence of Worship"

*In the following sermon excerpt, John Wimber lays out his understanding of the Trinitarian basis of worship (i.e., what the respective roles of God the Father, the Son, and the Holy Spirit are in Christian worship). He explains that worship is made possible only by the redeeming work of Jesus Christ and the activity of the Holy Spirit. Wimber's evangelical piety is demonstrated in speaking of Jesus Christ not only as the mediator of worship to the Father, but also as the recipient of worship. The word "worship" is so strongly connected to singing that the words are almost synonyms. Wimber is quick to note that Christians do not just sing, but engage in a "ministering" to God and, likewise, receive ministering from God. The excerpt begins with a quote from Hebrews.*

"... When Christ appeared as a high priest of the good things to come, he entered through the greater and more perfect tabernacle, not made with hands, that is to say, not of this creation; and not through the blood of goats and calves, but through his own blood. He entered the holy place once and for all, having obtained eternal redemption. For if the blood of goats and bulls and the ashes of a heifer sprinkling those who have been defiled sanctify for the cleansing of the flesh, how much more will the blood of Christ, who through the eternal Spirit offered himself without blemish to God, cleanse your conscience from dead works to serve the living God?"[9]

You see, it's the blood of Jesus that makes it possible for us to worship God the way we do. It's the blood of Jesus that has opened the way for you and I to have an intimate relationship with God the Father. That we might enter into the Holy of Holies, enter into the tabernacle of God. Because Jesus, our high priest, is not only our high priest, but he's our sacrifice and he's paid the way. So when we bow our heads or lift our heads or bow our knee or stand up or lay down or whatever posture we get into physically and we do it out of obedience to God, out of love for God, out of adoration for God based on the understanding that we're to worship him and him alone and that he is our provision, that he has provided us all that we have and that he is, in him everything that we ever will be or ever hope to be. When we understand those things and we come into his presence and we say, "Lord Jesus, because of your blood, I can enter into the Holy of Holies and speak directly to the Father," we're doing the very thing that God designed us for and so we're not just singing songs. We're ministering unto the Lord. We're talking to him and sharing our love with him and he with us and us with him.

Look at the 10th chapter, 19th verse [of Hebrews]. This is a little caption onto what I've just told you: "Since therefore, brethren, we have confidence to enter the holy place by the blood of Jesus, by a new and living way which he inaugurated for us through the veil, that is, his flesh, and since we have a great priest over the house of God, let us draw near with a sincere heart in full assurance of faith, having our hearts sprinkled clean from an evil conscience and our bodies washed with pure water. Let us hold fast the confession of our hope without wavering, for he who promised is faithful; and let us consider how to stimulate one another to love and good deeds, not forsaking our own assembling together (coming together to worship), as is the habit of some, but encouraging one another; and all the more as you see the day drawing near." Isn't that a beautiful passage?

And it's dealing with the essential fact and reality that we've entered into a relationship

The phrases "to worship God" and "to have an intimate relationship with God" seem to be synonymous. The connection between the two is one of the central aspects of the Vineyard approach to worship.

Wimber wants the congregation to be able to discern rightly what truly is happening during the extended time of singing. His interpretation puts the emphasis not on the worshiper's enjoyment of the songs but on God; singing in worship is active ministering to God.

9. Wimber is reading from Hebrews 9:11-14, New American Standard Version.

with Jesus Christ. We've entered into a relationship with the Father through the Son because he has broken the veil. Remember the veil in the temple that separated the high priest from God, that only the priest could go into the temple and only after he had done certain washings and gone through certain ceremonies and that he went in there to represent the people and to plead the people's case before God. Well, Jesus has taken it all out of the way. The curtain is rent. The temple is open now. The very throne, the living place of God, is available to you and I.

So when we worship, we're not just singing songs. We're entering into the Holy of Holies and ministering unto the Lord and he unto us. So we worship God on the grounds of that shed blood of Jesus. That's the only grounds that we can come to him on.

One more thing . . . we worship God by the Spirit of God. Let's go back to Philippians again, third chapter, first three verses: "Finally, my brethren, rejoice in the Lord. To write the same things again is no trouble to me. And it's a safeguard for you. Beware of the dogs, beware of the evil workers, beware of the false circumcision; for we are the true circumcision. . . ." Now keep in mind the rite of circumcision in the Old Testament was performed on the male child, I think eight days, something like that, eight days, is that right? Yeah. And that it was the mark of his birthright as an Israelite, but in the New Testament we have a circumcision also. It's not a physical circumcision; now it's a spiritual circumcision. It's a circumcision of the heart. Paul develops this at length in the book of Romans so that we can have an understanding of how we've entered into this relationship with God. In this spiritual circumcision is a circumcision in which our hearts have been quickened to the presence and the reality and the provision of God. It's one in which we in a major sense fall in love with Jesus Christ and have an intimate love relationship with him. [Philippians 3:3-4] says, "we are the true circumcision, who worship in the Spirit of God and glory in Christ Jesus and put no confidence in the flesh, although I myself might have confidence. . . . If anyone else has a mind to put confidence in the flesh, I far more." Then he goes on and tells, gives you a story [about his impeccable Jewish background]. But he says that ain't where it's at. He says our confidence in our worship is in Christ Jesus and our worship is through and by and in the Spirit of God.

Look at John the fourth chapter again. Remember, you don't have to turn to it, just let me remind you of it. This is the woman at the well, Samaritan lady. And Jesus says, "God is a spirit,[10] and they that worship him must worship him in spirit and truth" [John 4:24]. So our worship is by and in and through the Spirit of God. By and in and through the work of Jesus Christ and his shed blood to the Father and the Son.

Wimber expands the notion of worship "ministry" by noting that God is not merely the passive recipient of adoration. Being present with his people, God responds with power. Thus Vineyard worship was characterized by expecting God "to show up" and to act.

This transforming, renewing work of the Holy Spirit in the human heart appears to be a pre-condition for true worship in Wimber's understanding.

Strong affective language and images of person-to-person attachment can attract worshipers to Jesus, the most "concrete" of the Persons of the Trinity.

---

Source: John Wimber, "Essence of Worship," in *The Ministry and Teachings of John Wimber* series, CD #311 (Doin' the Stuff/Vineyard Music Group, 2004). Used by permission: Sean and Christy Wimber, 2015 @ Yorba Linda Vineyard/Wimber. Global.

10. It appears that Wimber might have made an inadvertent slip of the tongue. Many English translations of the Bible have "God is spirit" although the King James Version has "God is a spirit."

# Theology of Worship Documents

## Outline of Vineyard Teaching

*The chart below is excerpted from a worship seminar handbook distributed in the 1980s through Anaheim Vineyard, originally developed by Carl Tuttle and Ralph Kucera. It uses biblical examples to indicate the variety of ways Christians should worship. Note the method of reading the Scriptures by studying various words for "worship." The method seems to place a stronger emphasis upon worship as individual activity rather than on the church's collected activity in that the biblical examples seem to focus on individuals more than the whole people of God. The document comes from a private collection of a participant. Having to rely upon such a source indicates another difficulty with respect to studying this congregation and John Wimber. Unlike older movements and long-departed figures, the systematic gathering and archiving of relevant historical materials is in its first stages.*

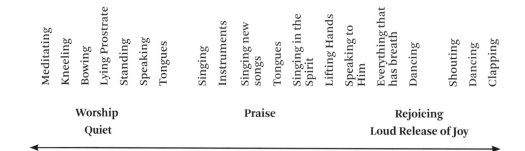

|  |  |  |
|---|---|---|
| **Worship** | **Praise** | **Rejoicing** |
| Quiet | | **Loud Release of Joy** |

C.  Earthly expressions by God's saints

This explanation of worship uses a strong emphasis on biblical words for worship and examples of worship from the Bible. The approach is not speculative or theoretical.

1.  Musical worship/praise *(zamar,* zaw-mar)

    a.  Singing to Him (Psalm 147:1,7, Colossians 3:16)

        (1)  Choruses, hymns, psalms

        (2)  A basic level—[it] can become mechanical

    b.  Instrumental praise/worship *(zamar,* zaw-mar)

        (1)  Types: brass, stringed, percussion, wind/reed (Psalm 150:3–5)

        (2)  Effects

            (a)  Banishes darkness (1 Samuel 16:14–16, 22–23),

            (b)  Invites God's *ministering* presence (2 Kings 3:1–16, 2 Chronicles 29:25, 5:11–14)

    c.  "Everything that has breath" (Psalm 150:6)

        Musical: non-verbal, melodies or harmonies

    d.  Singing new songs (Psalm 144:9)

        (1)  Most intimate expression

        (2)  Personal, first person, intimate adoration

        (3)  *Spirit-inspired* songs from our hearts

        (4)  Direct (not memorized or learned) expressions of faith

        (5)  Can be done with our minds or spirit (1 Corinthians 14:15)

One normally gives liturgical instruction or correctives only for situations that actually exist within a congregation. Here Tuttle and Kucera are addressing some of the more ecstatic dimensions of early Vineyard worship: speaking in tongues and shouting.

2.  Vocal worship/praise/rejoicing

    a.  Speaking of His greatness and goodness

        (1)  Eagerly utter, bubble over with joy

        (2)  Psalm 145:6–7, 11–13, 21

    b.  Speaking with other tongues (languages)

        (1)  Holy Spirit—our spirit—God

        (2)  Analogous to a river of worship/praise/rejoicing

        (3)  Speaking of God's mighty deeds (Acts 2:11)

        (4)  Glorifying God (Acts 2:11)

        (5)  Giving thanks (1 Corinthians 14:17).

    c.  Shouting joyfully to Him (Psalm 47:1; Ezra 3:10–13)

    (1) Not noises or screams; loudly spoken praises

    (2) Purpose: expresses His triumph (1 Thessalonians 4:16)

    (3) Effects of joyful shouting

        (a) Breaks down barriers, puts us into contact with Him (Joshua 6:5)

        (b) Psalm 89:15: A blessing for those who know the joyful shout

        (c) Banishes clouds of oppression, [so] that we might receive from the Son!

3. Presenting our bodies (Romans 12:1)

    a. Lifting up holy hands

        (1) Nehemiah 8:6; 1 Timothy 2:8

        (2) Thanksgiving, surrender, dependence

        (3) Offering up our hearts (Lamentations 3:40)

    b. Kneeling (Psalm 95:6–7)

        (1) Humility, meekness, submission

        (2) Blessing Him (literal Hebrew meaning)

        (3) Earnestness (Luke 5:8)

    c. Bowing low with our faces to the ground

        (1) Nehemiah 8:6; Genesis 18:2; Psalm 95:6–7

        (2) Fear, respect, reverence

    d. Lying prostrate or falling on our faces

        (1) Revelation 1:10–17; Numbers 14:5; 16:22, 45; Daniel 8:17; Ezekiel 1:28, 44:4.

        (2) Total awe, fear, reverence

    e. Standing in His presence (Psalm 134:1; Deuteronomy 10:8). Acknowledgment of royalty; service

    f. Clapping our hands (Psalm 47:1). Releasing of joy and thanksgiving.

    g. Dancing before Him (Ezekiel 15:17–21; 2 Samuel 6:14–15; Psalm 149:3; 150:4)

        (1) Releasing of joy, thanksgiving, celebration of His victoriousness [sic]

        (2) Types of dancing

            (a) *Karar:* to move quickly, twirl (2 Samuel 6:14–16)

            (b) *Mecholah* or *machol:* a company or round dance (Exodus 15:20; Jeremiah 31:4, 13; Psalm 149:3; 150:4)

            (c) *Raqad:* to leap, skip about, jump, spring about wildly (1 Chronicles 15:29); "dancing in the Spirit"

4. Renewing our minds (Romans 12:2)

    a. Hebrew words for meditation

        (1) *Hagah* (haw-gaw) (Joshua 1:8): To meditate upon Meditation-obedience-prosperous path-wisdom

        (2) *Siyach* (see-akh) (Psalm 119:15): To ponder, (by implication) converse with oneself (Psalm 119:9–14)

Although in slightly different form, Wimber's insistence that true biblical worship involves the whole person—body, mind, and spirit—can be found in this outline. Compare the presentation here to his preaching in the sermon "Loving God" (pp. 87-102).

   b. Christian meditation: involves filling your mind with God, His goodness and beauty; it involves a detachment (from the world) and an attachment (to God). It is inner communion with Him (listening to Him-speaking to Him). It involves wholeness of personhood or individuality.

   c. Pagan meditation: involves emptying your mind, allowing for anything to enter your mind; detachment from the world. It involves a loss of personhood and individuality. It involves merging with the impersonal, cosmic mind. In Transcendental Meditation there are several stages or degrees from a "waking state" to "mind out of gear." This involves a person turning over his [sic] mind to something or someone other than himself.

   d. Types of meditation

     (1) Long continuous thinking (Psalm 143:5; 145:5; 77)

     (2) Muse: ponder, wonder, seeking why (Psalm 143:5; 77)

     (3) Remember: recalling to mind (Psalm 143:5; 1 Chronicles 16:12, 15)

     (4) Relax: being still before Him (Psalm 46:10; 4:4–5)

   e. Focuses of meditation

     (1) God's Person (Psalm 62:5)

     (2) God's Word: The Scriptures (Psalm 1:1–2)

     (3) God's works (Psalm 77:12)

     (4) Past victories (Psalm 143:5, Lamentations 3:21–23)

     (5) God's beauty: creation's beauty (Philippians 4:8)

   f. Meditation exercises[1]

     (1) *Celebration of Discipline* by Richard Foster "Palms up, palms down"

       (a) Palms up—receiving from Him.

       (b) Palms down—casting away burdens (Psalm 55:22; 1 Peter 5:7).

       (c) This keeps us current with God.

     (2) *Alone with God* by Campbell McAlpine

       Scripture meditation: internalizing and personalizing God's word

     (3) *The Other Side of Silence* by Morton Kelsey

       Imagination: creating scenes (memories) of intimacy with God; transporting yourself into scriptural narratives

---

Source: Carl Tuttle and Ralph Kucera, Worship Seminar outline handout (no date), pp. 16-18. Used with permission.

1. Mention is made of three books which provide guidance on contemplative prayer exercises: Richard J. Foster's *Celebration of Discipline: The Path to Spiritual Growth* (first published in 1978), Campbell McAlpine's *Alone with God: A Manual of Biblical Meditation* (1981), and Morton Kelsey's *The Other Side of Silence: A Guide to Christian Meditation* (1976).

## *Wimber's Understanding of Worship as God-Given Destiny*

*In this essay, John Wimber explains the God-centeredness that he believes is appropriate for Christian worship. He also discusses the calling to become a true worshiper.*

Becoming true worshipers is the chief assignment God has given us in this lifetime. I believe that God is bringing the church to her knees to teach her how to express her love to Him in intimate, loving and adoring language.

In addition, the Lord calls us to live a life of worship. The Word, our walk with Christ and the works of the church as a whole are all expressions of worship. They necessarily flow out of hearts that are devoted to the Lord.

Developing intimacy in worship takes time. For some, it is easy to get side-tracked or annoyed by the person sitting next to you whose expression in worship may be more exuberant and free than you are comfortable with. Some people are tempted to think, "I'll never learn to be this expressive with my body or hands." Let me tell you, I never thought I would be! But you will. You will either learn to worship Him intimately now here on earth or later in heaven, because worship is what heaven is all about.

Worship is not about personality, temperament, personal limitations, or church background—it's about God. We are called to do it for his benefit, not ours. Yet the irony is that we do indeed benefit greatly when we give ourselves to worshiping God. We've been designed to worship.

> The image of worship as intimacy with God gives Wimber the place to address taking the time to learn how to participate fully and well, a common, recurring issue in learning a new way of worship.

---

Source: John Wimber, "The Life-Changing Power of Worship," in *All About Worship: Insights and Perspectives on Worship* (Anaheim, CA: Vineyard Music Group, 1998), 6. Used with permission.

## *Wimber Teaches Worship as Abandonment to God*

*In teaching, John Wimber would use the story of the woman from John 12:1–8 to illustrate complete abandonment to God in worship. This abandonment applies both to corporate worship and everyday living. This emphasis upon worship as a way of life helps balance the intense experience of worship often experienced in a Vineyard Fellowship with practical acts of service in the world.*

"Then Mary took about a pint of pure nard, an expensive perfume; she poured it on Jesus' feet and wiped his feet with her hair. And the house was filled with the fragrance of the perfume." [John 12:3, NIV]

Every time I choose to do things God's way and resist my way, I think my spirit is kneeling in front of Jesus and I am pouring sweet perfume on His feet and wiping them with my hair. . . .

See page 83 to compare this description with John Wimber's song "Sweet Perfume."

Our entire life can be worship to God. All the pain and the times of sorrow can be surrendered in an act of worship with just as much value as the spontaneous praise and gratitude that goes up when we experience the joy and blessings of life.

Every act of obedience is worship. Every time we choose another over ourselves, it is an act of worship. Every time we decide to lay our own way down in favor of Jesus' way, is an act of worship. . . .

The word worship in its simplest form means, "to serve." . . . As you live out your life, who are you going to serve? In the hundreds of little choices you make every day, who are you choosing to serve? . . . Will I be kind to my spouse, my sister, and my neighbor and thereby give my worship to God, or will I consider myself the most important person in the exchanges and therefore worship myself?

Will I joyfully give in to inconvenience when it's required as an act of worship, or will I demand my place and worship myself?

Will I love even when the other is unlovable and let that be an act of worship? Or will I "Amen" the spirit of this world and make my life's pursuit reaching my full potential?

If we worship Jesus, therefore serving Him, then our every act and thought has meaning. Acts of kindness are not just little niceties, they become acts of worship. Bagging food for the poor because "I was hungry and you gave me food" [see Matt. 25:35] is worship.

Every time you make the decision to walk in truth and humility, every time you put someone else ahead of you, every time you decide to pray for someone who has hurt or offended you instead of hating them, it is an act of worship. It's all worship!

. . . "Sacrifice and offering you did not desire, but my ears you have pierced, burnt offerings and sin offerings you did not require. Then I said, 'Here I am, I have come. It is written about me in the scroll. I desire to do your will, O my God, your law is within my heart'" (Psalm 40:6–7).

Here David prophesies about Jesus, and the author of Hebrews takes this up, talking about Jesus and His attitude of worship towards His Father: "I have come to do your will, not my will but yours be done." [See Luke 22:42.]

What does the reference "piercing the ear" mean? It was a sign that you belonged to another, and your life was no longer your own. It meant that you have a master you love and you chose to live with him instead of going out on your own. . . .

Worship is not only singing or the experience of God in singing; it is a life lived in obedience to God's will as exemplified by Jesus Christ.

Worship is how you live. It's where and how you spend your time and your money. Worship manifests in obedience. As you worship in obedience, your life here has meaning and purpose. This is called a lifestyle of worship to the King!

---

Source: John Wimber, *The Way In Is the Way On* (Atlanta: Ampelon Publishing, 2006), 113-17. Used with permission.

## Teaching on the Corporate Nature of Worship

*Notwithstanding the intensely personal and intimate nature of the experience of worship in the congregation, Wimber sought to reinforce a sense of the collective corporate nature of worship as an activity of the whole church and all its members. The following two passages from 1983 sermons speak to this issue. Note especially in the second passage his disdain for services that have turned into entertainment spectacles.*

But it [worship] is the first order of the Church. When we begin studying the topic, we find out that it is God's highest priority. When Jesus was talking to the woman at the well, probably one of the most important texts in the whole New Testament is communicated when He responded to her and said, "The Father seeks such to worship Him" [John 4:23]. In what way? Well, the preceding sentence says, "That the hour will come, and now is in which those who worship Him, worship in spirit and truth." I remember four years ago pondering over that text. "What did the Lord mean?" The Lord finally gave me the revelation, the understanding that He meant Himself. That He was the truth and via the Spirit of God we could literally worship in Him. His intention was to draw all people together in one Body, the Body of Jesus Christ, that Body that we are a part of, and that we would be taught to worship Him and that that would be the primary aim of the Church. Beginning to study that topic in the Scripture, it became apparent to me all the time that that is what God had intended from the very outset.

. . . We said last week that many people in the church today are an audience, rather than an army [of God]. And by that, I mean that many churches are operating on an assembly kind of understanding that is really more theatrical than it is Biblical. They literally buy time in the newspaper and time on the radio, and they advertise, and they draw a crowd. And the crowd comes together, and they put on a spectacle. They get people up on a platform, and the people do the kinds of things that people do up on a platform to entertain crowds. They call that "Church," [but] that is a crowd. There is a difference between a crowd and a Church. Just as there is a difference between a convert and a disciple, an audience and an army.

Do some people come to your church expecting to be entertained? What are the features of your service—or of this Vineyard congregation—that could subtly create an audience mentality?

Source: Excerpts from pages 2 and 10 respectively of presentations entitled "Worship" and "Discipleship" in "Basic Priorities of Vineyard Christian Fellowship," Box 13, John Wimber Collection, Regent University Library Archives, Virginia Beach, Virginia. Used with permission.

## The Church's Pragmatism Shapes Planning

*Like many American churches with Pentecostal or charismatic roots, the Anaheim Vineyard was a combination of both a desire to replicate the power and experience of the biblical church and a pragmatic organizing for effective ministry. In other words, this congregation's ministry was neither pure power from miracle nor simply affect from music; it was careful planning leavened by pragmatism.[2] The internal planning documents of the budding congregation already show a clear sense of defined mission and practice along this line, including its sense of who its target or "market" will be, as these 1980 excerpts show. These documents likely show Wimber's background as a Church Growth consultant.*

I. The Mission: The five-year organization plan for Calvary Chapel, Yorba Linda-Placentia will enable us to implement and continue the following:

   A. To reach this generation for Jesus Christ.

   B. To minister beginning in Northeast Orange County and extending through our Jerusalem-Judea, Samaria to the uttermost parts of the world.

   C. To minister to a select group of people that here and after will be called the "rock" generation people. These people are not necessarily rock adherents, but they are people that have been heavily influenced by and have been raised in the thirty year period between the advent of rock and roll in the early '50s through 1980.

      1. The Need

        a. What is the need that this organization will meet? (National Vision)

          1. This church provides a church model which is compatible to a life style of a high percentage of people in the United States that might be called "church drop-outs." These people are primarily "believers who do not belong and are people who do not like the confines of denominationalism. Therefore, a church that can focus on this market has a great opportunity for growth in the United States today.

          2. This church could provide a viable leadership model to a work force that is known to us across the United States, made up primarily of people who for one reason or another are disillusioned with the church structure and institutionalism of today. These people are of Bible school [age] or above. They have either dropped out or are contemplating dropping out of the denominational church ministry. (Local Vision)

          3. To meet the needs of such people as the above in the Northern Orange County area.

          4. To establish a strong "relational" fellowship that would provide not only a model for national transference but a satisfactory life-style

---

Evangelicals often use the Jerusalem-Judea-Samaria phrasing, based on Acts 1:8, as shorthand for a sense of witnessing for Christ both locally and globally.

In 1992, Donald Miller, a University of Southern California sociologist, reported on a survey of about 1,300 members that 18 percent of the Anaheim Vineyard members claimed no prior religious affiliation before joining this congregation. Source: Box 18, John Wimber Collection, Regent University Library Archives, Virginia Beach, Virginia.

---

2. This useful categorization is based on Grant Wacker's discussion of primitivism and pragmatism in *Heaven Below: Early Pentecostals and American Culture* (Cambridge: Harvard University Press, 2001).

supporting the biblical values that are essential for a New Testament type church. . . .

3. Assumptions (Policy as guidelines to keep us on target)

   a. Organizational Assumptions

      1. Organization will follow a "Spirit led" ministry.

      2. Organization will always be negotiable.

      3. Positions in the organization are directly related to function, not status.

   b. Market

     Our market is the "Rock" generation young people to middle-aged, approximately fourteen to twenty million un-churched "believers who do not belong" in the United States. . . .

> Is it helpful or dangerous to use market language to speak of those whom a church wishes to reach?

5. The Scope

   a. Our first objective is to establish a church in Northeastern Orange County.

   b. Our second objective is to grow it to 8,000 totally involved by 1985.

   c. To establish either by renting, leasing or purchase a facility that can accommodate such.

   d. To establish a church planting agency that can begin planting churches in the immediate area and throughout the country.

   e. To establish a music-arts ministry that would train leadership for musical groups for Christian nurture as well as evangelism.

> Since this outline is excerpted from the original to include only sections dealing directly with worship, a few sections, such as 2 and 4, have been intentionally left out.

6. Priorities

   a. Worship: To give God's love back to Him in worship. Therefore: We give priority to the ministry of praise and song to the Lord.

   b. Fellowship: To give God's love to each other. Therefore: We give priority to the involvement of adults in Kinship groups for fellowship.

   c. Evangelism and social concern: To give God's love to the community sharing the Good News and caring for their needs.

> Is it surprising to find that the list of priorities has worship at the top? What would be the list of priorities at your church?

---

Source: "Calvary Chapel Yorba Linda/Placentia Five Year Plan 1980-1985," Box 19, John Wimber Collection, Regent University Library Archives, Virginia Beach, Virginia, pages 1-2, 4, 6. Used with permission.

## The Phases of Worship

*Explanation of the Vineyard way of worship developed as the 1980s progressed. After the mantle of worship leader shifted from Carl Tuttle to Eddie Espinosa around 1983, John Wimber began* *teaching about the **five phases of worship**. This teaching, which reflected the congregation's emerging worship patterns and ideas that had been circulating in Pentecostalism more broadly, arose out of interactions between Epinosa and Wimber in the mid-1980s. A sense of progressing through experiential stages in worship shapes the musician's understanding of which songs to sing and in what order to place them. Attentiveness to a song's content, emotional tone, and the cumulative effect of the musical set likely become the key considerations in this approach.*

This Vineyard approach is only one of the models that proponents of extended musical sets use to explain the set's proper role and organization. Another common explanation is to think of the prolonged period of worship music as a journey through the various areas of the Old Testament tabernacle or temple. The goal is entering into God's presence in the innermost sanctum, the Holy of Holies.

In the Vineyard we see five basic phases of worship, phases through which leaders attempt to lead the congregation. Understanding these phases is helpful in our experience of God. Keep in mind that as we pass through these phases we are headed toward one goal: intimacy with God. I define intimacy as belonging to or revealing one's deepest nature to another (in this case to God), and it is marked by close association, presence, and contact. . . .

The first phase is the call to worship, which is a message directed toward the people or toward God. It is an invitation to worship. This might be accomplished through a song like "Come, Let Us Worship and Bow Down."[3] Or it may be jubilant, such as through the song "Don't You Know It's Time to Praise the Lord?"[4]

The underlying thought of the call to worship is "Let's do it, let's worship now." Song selection for the call to worship is quite important, for this sets the tone for the gathering and directs people to God. . . .

The second phase is the engagement, which is the electrifying dynamic of connection to God and to each other. Expressions of love, adoration, praise, jubilation, intercession, petition—all of the dynamics of prayer are interlocked with worship—come forth from one's heart. In the engagement phase we praise God for who he is through music as well as prayer. An individual may have moments like these in his or her private worship at home, but when the church comes together the manifest presence of God is magnified and multiplied.

As we move further in the engagement phase, we move more and more into a loving and intimate language. Being in God's presence excites our hearts and minds and we want to praise him for the deeds he has done, for how he has moved in history, for his character and attributes. . . .

Often this intimacy causes us to meditate, even as we are singing, on our relationship with the Lord. Sometimes we recall vows we have made before our God. God might call to our minds disharmony or failure in our lives, thus confession of sin is involved. Tears may flow as we see our disharmony but his harmony; our limitations but his unlimited possibilities. This phase in which we have been awakened to his presence is called expression.

3. Wimber may be referring to a song by this title written by Dave Doherty and copyrighted in 1980 by Universal Music—Brentwood Benson Publishing.

4. This song is likely one written by Bruce and Judi Borneman and copyrighted in 1981 by Maranatha! Music. The second verse speaks of the Lord dwelling within the praises of his people. This idea, based on Psalm 22:3 and similar scriptures, becomes a popular motif among "contemporary" worshipers.

Physical and emotional expression in worship can result in dance and body movement. This is an appropriate response to God if the church is on that crest. It is inappropriate if it is whipped up or if the focal point is on the dance rather than on true jubilation in the Lord. . . .

Expression then moves to a zenith, a climactic point, not unlike physical lovemaking (doesn't Solomon use the same analogy in the Song of Songs?). We have expressed what is in our hearts and minds and bodies, and now it is time to wait for God to respond. Stop talking and wait for him to speak, to move. I call this, the fourth phase, visitation: The almighty God visits his people.

His visitation is a byproduct of worship. We don't worship in order to gain his presence. He is worthy to be worshiped whether or not he visits us. But God "dwells in the praises of his people." [See Psalm 22:3.] So we should always come to worship prepared for an audience with the King.

The church must be quickened to the fact that the God of the universe will visit us if we but worship him in spirit and truth. Much of the time when Christians come together they don't expect God to do much. But God is like an anxious bridegroom outside the bride's door. And we, as the bride, frequently forget what we are there for because we are scattered in our thoughts or preoccupied with concerns.

We should expect the Spirit of God to work among us. He moves in different ways—sometimes for salvation, sometimes for deliverances, sometimes for sanctification or healings. God also visits through the prophetic gifts. Often the genuine prophets are too timid to speak up. The Lord needs to deepen us in the prophetic gifts. He visits us through Spirit-inspired Scripture reading which has a prophetic meaning for that moment. Exhortation—that is, a word of encouragement—can be given this way. We need to learn to wait on the Lord and let him speak.

The fifth phase of worship is the giving of substance. The church knows so little about giving, yet the Bible exhorts us to give to God. It is pathetic to see people preparing for ministry who don't know how to give. That is like an athlete entering a race, yet he doesn't know how to run. If we haven't learned to give money, we haven't learned anything. Ministry is a life of giving. We give our whole lives; God should have ownership of everything. Remember, whatever we give God control of he can multiply and bless, not so we can amass goods, but so we can be more involved in his enterprise.

Whatever I need to give, God inevitably first calls me to give it when I don't have any of it—whether it is money, love, hospitality, or information. Whatever God wants to give through us he first has to do to us. We are the first partaker of the fruit. But we are not to eat the seed, we are to sow it to give it away.

The underlying premise is that whatever we are is multiplied, for good or for bad. Whatever we have on our tree is what we are going to get in our orchard.

Compare this developed model of the phases of worship to the statements of Carl Tuttle found toward the beginning of this book that there was no pre-established set list of songs originally. Wimber's teaching here appears to be an explanation based on natural development as this congregation settled into a way of worship. Do you think Wimber's description of the phases of worship here is more descriptive of his congregation's worship or prescriptive for others? Or both?

As we experience these phases of worship, we experience intimacy with God, the highest and most fulfilling calling men and women may know.

———————

Source: John Wimber, "Worship: Intimacy with God," in *Thoughts on Worship* (Anaheim, CA: Vineyard Music Group, 1996), 4-7. See also John Wimber, *The Way In Is the Way On* (Atlanta: Ampelon Publishing, 2006), 121-24. Used with permission.

## *Reflections on Musicians and the Difficulty of Their Role*

*Given music's importance in Vineyard worship, music leaders could be under particular strains and temptations. Not surprisingly, John Wimber and other Vineyard teachers gave thought to the proper character for a church musician. Considering the appropriate disposition of a musician before the Lord was an important element in the Vineyard's theology of worship. In the 1990s, John Wimber was interviewed by Stuart Townend, a British songwriter. In the interview, Wimber reflects on the best preparation to lead worship as well as his own spiritual journey.*

Question: As writers, musicians and worship leaders, then, how should we prepare for what God has in store for us?

John: The difficulty will not be so much in the writing of new and great music; the test will be in the godliness of those that perform and deliver it. In that sense some of our worship community is not well prepared for revival. Many have been allowed into worship leading because of this new emphasis on contemporary groups and music, and the consequent need for their worship skills and musical skills. But little has been said to them about the need for godliness, spirituality and depths of maturity in their individual and family lives. Quite frankly, many of our musicians are just not steeped in a daily spirituality.

We learned a lot from our own experiences of God's initial outpouring in the Vineyard in 1979, and the following years. In that period we had both blessing and destruction. We had people that were just not ready to be used by God in a highly public way, although you would have thought they were from their gifts of teaching, ministry or music: they were very gifted, they just weren't very godly.

Having worked as a pastor for a number of years, my concern in this current wave is that we all get through this thing with marriages, families and churches intact, so that we can "give a good report to God in that day. . . ."

*In the interview, Wimber recounts the importance and permanence of surrendering his life, including his music, to Christ back in 1963. This laying down of his own agenda set the pattern for the rest of his life and the ideal to which he called other musicians.*

> Do congregations ever overlook these qualities (godliness and maturity) when enamored of technically great music?

> Wimber is alluding to stories from the Gospels where the point of Christian living and ministry is to achieve a good report when Christ returns.

Question: So if we want to keep in step with what God's doing, and be available to be used by Him, how can we practically set about it?

John: . . . I've preached many times that we are called to a reverential serving of God with our whole heart and being, stressing that if anything except God is your portion in life, I can't guarantee it: I can't guarantee that your children will be happy, or that your spouse will love you forever. . . . But I can guarantee that if your desire is Jesus, you'll get Jesus, and you can walk with Him all the days of your life.

When I went through cancer a year or so ago, I was astonished when people from my own church asked me, "Weren't you afraid you were going to die?" After about the fifteenth person, I realized I hadn't really taught my congregation the truth of the Word. I had to get to them and say, "In June of 1963, this man died. And everything from that time to this has been Jesus." I'm not trying to hold onto my life: I gave my life up. When I became a Christian, I was a musician with two albums I had produced in the U.S. Top Ten; it was the establishment of my career after thirteen years of hard work. But God spoke to me in the two-line parable of the pearl of great price: "I want it, give it to me." [See Matt. 13:45–46.] He didn't say, "Give it to me and I will give you a career as a pastor, or music that will go to many nations of the world." He said, "Give me everything. Liquidate all your assets, and I will give you the pearl."

Now the pearl isn't a new career, or the opportunity to make a name for yourself as a worship writer or leader. It isn't even the ability to sustain yourself in that profession. If your readers' motivation in being involved in their local church worship is to make a full-time career of it, they'll probably be disappointed.

The pearl is Jesus.

---

Source: These reflections were originally published as "The Musician in Revival," *Worship Together* 10 (1994): 5-6, and were reprinted in John Wimber, *The Way In Is the Way On* (Atlanta: Ampelon Publishing, 2006), 127-30. Used with permission.

Wimber's thoughts here come from the 1990s, toward the end of his life, and reflect how critical the chief musician—a "worship leader"—had become in Vineyard and other forms of "contemporary" worship. His thoughts reflect a temptation that arises through the important role the musician had in this way of worship. The term "worship leader" was used very little in the materials in this book dating from the 1970s and early 1980s.

## Outsider Concerns about the Miraculous

*Occasionally concerns arose about John Wimber's emphasis upon signs and wonders, including healing. One hot spot was the course, which he team-taught at Fuller Seminary starting in 1982, which looked at the role of the miraculous in Christian ministry. At the time the course broke all enrollment records at Fuller, and the ministry sessions held at the end of class attracted overflow crowds of nonstudents. But questions arose within and beyond the school. A moratorium was declared on the course, and a faculty task force studied the class in order to draft a report, which was published as a book entitled* Ministry and the Miraculous: A Case Study at Fuller Theological Seminary *and edited by Fuller professor Lewis B. Smedes. In the foreword, Fuller president*

*David Allan Hubbard summarized the theological and pastoral points found in the published report. These points seem to serve as a kind of review of the tensions that often arose when outsiders considered the emphasis upon healing and other supernatural events in the life of the early Vineyard. Others at the time raised similar issues.* [5]

What our task force has ventured, and what our faculty has received and affirmed, treats subjects of concern to thousands of pastors and tens of thousands of laypersons. The tack that it takes between the shoals of denying the possibility of miracles in our day and the rocks of presumption that demand miracles according to our need and schedule seems the way of wisdom for the entire church. The discussion of differences of world view and their bearing on how we view the supernatural will open new vistas for many. The survey of the ways in which the Creator may work his healing will enlarge our perspective on God and evoke our praises of his name. The thorny matter of the verification of claims to the miraculous is not bypassed; exuberance at the expense of truthfulness is shown to be no spiritual bargain. Finally the role of pain in Christian discipleship is explored, and the miracle of grace to bear pain is valued alongside the miracle of grace that eases pain.

What are appropriate, reasonable, and scriptural expectations for seeing dramatic works of God's Spirit in the world today?

Source: Lewis B. Smedes, ed., *Ministry and the Miraculous: A Case Study at Fuller Theological Seminary* (Pasadena, CA: Fuller Theological Seminary, 1987), 17. Used with permission.

5. See, for example, the sidebar entitled "Cause for Concern" by Ben Patterson in Tim Stafford, "Testing the Wine from John Wimber's Vineyard," *Christianity Today* 30, no. 11 (August 8, 1986): 20.

# PART THREE

# ASSISTING THE INVESTIGATION

# Why Study Anaheim Vineyard's Worship? Suggestions for Devotional Use

The following are suggestions for devotional use that correspond with specific sections of the book.

## Describing Anaheim Vineyard's Worship

- The lyrics by the group Love Song speak about the positive change that God had brought to the people in their church: "Lookin' past the hair and straight into the eyes." Pray for the guidance and forgiveness of the Spirit of God for occasions when you might have stumbled by judging fellow worshipers by their physical appearance.
- The "giving of substance" was the last phase of worship as taught in the Anaheim Vineyard congregation. There is edginess to the teaching in that it seeks to subvert self-centeredness in worship. Consider whether you have allowed the enjoyment of worship experience to become an end in itself. Read slowly about the prophet's experience in Isaiah 6 to see how a wonderful experience of God might not be enjoyable and might lead to a call to minister to others.
- Reread the first-person descriptions of worship. How would you describe their response to worship? Describe a recent worship experience in a short paragraph. How did you see God at work as you worshiped? What emotions did you experience?

## People and Artifacts

- The images in this section show people with hands raised in worship. What words and emotions would you feel are best expressed in this posture? Position yourself in different postures as you pray. Do different postures encourage you to pray differently? If so, how?
- Over time, read through the Psalms. Try to visualize the tone of each Psalm as bodily posture. What range of positions and postures did you experience over time?

## *Worship Setting and Space*

- In the photographs in this section and in the ones in the "People and Artifacts" section, notice the proximity of worshipers to each other. The next time you worship be attentive to whoever is in front and to the rear of you. Be attentive to whoever is on either side. Pray for these persons at the beginning, in the middle, and at the end of the service.

## *Descriptions of Worship*

- What do you expect when you come to worship? Ask yourself whether you have grown complacent about expecting anything from God during a worship service. Pray to discern the reason for the loss of expectation.
- The worship descriptions speak often about the power of songs directed to God. Pick a song or two from your congregation's repertoire that directly addresses God in prayer. Consider carefully the words. Which biblical person could you imagine singing this song? For which biblical story would the song be fitting? Did this connection of current song and biblical episode open up new dimensions of the scriptural story?
- In reading the firsthand accounts of worship, one will notice the recurring emphasis upon the Holy Spirit. To gain a clearer sense of the Spirit's relationship to God the Father and the Lord Jesus Christ, read the letters of the Apostle Paul over time. Look for passages, e.g., Romans 8, in which two or three of the Persons are mentioned in close proximity. What is the Spirit's relationship to God the Father and to Jesus Christ?

## *Order of Service and Texts*

- Many of the songs used in the Vineyard make simple, direct affirmations. Consider meeting face-to-face with Jesus Christ. What three simple affirmations would you want to make to him?
- The first line of the first verse of Wimber's song entitled "Sweet Perfume" asks the worshiper to "consider how He (God) loves you." Read John 15:9 slowly, savoring each word. Contemplate how God the Father loves his Son, Jesus Christ. Write down your insights. Looking at what you have written, pray for the Holy Spirit to open your understanding to how Jesus Christ loves you.
- If you have an old songbook with lyrics to any of the songs in Anaheim Vineyard's song repertoire, read through one set of lyrics every day for a week. If you do not have a song-

book, choose songs mentioned in the texts and search the web for their lyrics. If the song is a prayer addressed to God, pray the lyrics as if you were speaking them to God.

## Sermons

- Consider John Wimber's assertion that, although he had attended church for a while, he had never learned to really worship. Contemplate that viewpoint. How did/do you learn to worship? Can or should people be taught to worship, or is it something that needs to be experienced? What is the value of reflecting on the worship experience afterward?
- For a week, pray two psalms a day. Remind yourself that God is truly interested and listening to what you are saying. As you reflect on the psalm, can you contemplate a deeper realization of being aware of God's love for you?
- Review your motivation for going to church and worship. Would you say it comes more from a sense of duty ("because I must"), a sense of delight ("because I delight in God"), or both? Or are there other motivations? How does love for God motivate you?
- In his preaching and teaching on worship, Wimber would remind worshipers that worship was not limited solely to the time called "worship," but should include all of life lived in a way to honor God. Consider in what ways you might have just been an "hour-or-two-a-week Christian," to use Wimber's phrase. Ask for God to forgive you and ask for the Spirit's strength to live life worshipfully. In what ways might your life change if you lived every moment in a way that honors God?

## Theology of Worship Documents

- Read slowly through the various documents in this section. Circle those attitudes, behaviors, and motivations regarding worshiping where you feel the most challenged. Praying for guidance, identify the most critical. Over a week, petition God to change these things in you.

# Why Study Anaheim Vineyard's Worship?
# Discussion Questions for Small Groups

Below you will find discussion questions for various sections of this book.

## General Introduction and Timeline

- Is there a relationship between the social turmoil of the 1960s and 1970s and the rise of worship renewal movements at the same time? Or is it just a coincidence?
- Some historians have suggested that identifying with a particular kind of music was an important feature of how Baby Boomers identified themselves with a social group. Do you think the same thing was going on in the new ways of worship arising in the 1970s? Why or why not?
- Why do you think some of the growing megachurches with new ways of worship developed publishing houses to record and distribute their music (i.e., Calvary Chapel with Maranatha! Music and Vineyard with Mercy Records), but others didn't?

## Describing the Community's Worship

- Many of the early Vineyard participants had been a part of another church before. Why do you think the 1960s, 1970s, and 1980s were a time when people might have switched church and denominational homes? What factors might contribute to this migration? What factors contribute to congregational loyalty?
- Music plays an important role in Vineyard's worship, especially as worshipers experience the presence of God. From your experience, what role does music play in Christian worship today?
- Usually when people think of "contemporary worship," they think of music. But is that the only thing that made Anaheim Vineyard's worship "contemporary" or "with the time"? For example, how might this congregation's worship be "with the time" in terms of atmosphere, dress, language, concerns, technology, or values? Can you think of other ways in which it was contemporary?
- Pastor John Wimber was involved strongly in the making of music in his congregation,

but that is not often the case. And so, "worship leader" usually has come to mean a musician. What does this development in terminology communicate about the roles of pastors and musicians in worship?

- One of the key desires in Vineyard worship is not only to sing *about* God but sing *to* God. Why might older pieces of music create the impression that they only talk about God? Is the impression a true one in your opinion?
- Consider the combination of images of God in Vineyard worship. What examples of an intimate, loving God can you find? What examples of an almighty, powerful God can you find?

## *People and Artifacts*

- Does the freedom to be expressive with one's body come from not having to handle books or texts when worshiping? What else may contribute to being free to be physically expressive?
- If you worship in an outwardly expressive church, is it your experience that a few people start with outward expression and then others follow? Do you think that is true from the pictures of the Vineyard fellowship? Is it surprising that it seems men are the first ones to express themselves outwardly on this occasion?
- The cover of one of the early Vineyard publications shows Old Testament characters worshiping. Is it important for Christians to feel like they are fulfilling worship in both the Old and New Testaments? Why or why not?

## *Worship Setting and Space*

- As you look through these images, do you think these spaces give a greater sense of God being present among the people or of God being a distant ruler? What features contribute to either sense?
- In worship, does the location of the musicians, in the midst of the congregation or somewhat distant in their own space, affect the experience? What are the advantages and disadvantages to both arrangements?
- This congregation first worshiped in homes and public buildings without a lot of church "fussiness," e.g., special furniture, decorations, and symbols. What is gained by that kind of environment, and what is lost?

## Descriptions of Worship

- Does it surprise you that early Vineyard worshipers most closely linked a sense of being in God's presence during the songs of intimate address to him? What kind of expectations do you think that creates for worship?
- Compared to the Anaheim Vineyard, would your church place more or less emphasis in worship upon the Holy Spirit?
- Many of the Anaheim Vineyard worshipers speak about coming to worship with a sense of vivid expectancy to encounter God. Do you think coming with a sense of expectancy is an important aspect of being prepared to worship well?
- Did the struggle some of the participants, including John Wimber, had with worship and participation in the music surprise you? What do you think might have given them trouble in initially participating well?

## Order of Service and Texts

- How many of the songs mentioned in the book did you know? What gives a song a short or long "shelf life"?
- In your opinion does the song repertoire of "contemporary worship" change too frequently or not frequently enough? Can you name good reasons for changing a congregation's song repertoire or for keeping it the same?
- Many of these songs have simple lyrics with a lot of repetition. Can you think of non-church examples of songs with the same features? What do these sorts of songs do well? For example, is it easier to move while singing, or is it easier to learn a song if you are not given the text? What are other strengths of such songs? What are possible downsides?

## Sermons

- John Wimber exhibited a winsome, attractive personality while preaching. In your opinion, how did Wimber's personality affect his listeners' ability to hear and accept his bold content?
- Wimber regularly reminded worshipers that worship was not about them but that it was about God. Why might worshipers continually fall into that trap of thinking worship was about them? Is it sinful nature? A consumerist attitude brought to worship? Perhaps even something built into a Vineyard worship service?

- Based on the sermons in this book, what do you think the central point of Wimber's preaching was if you had to summarize it?

## Theology of Worship Documents

- Wimber's teaching on worship repeatedly emphasized that worship should engage the whole human person in every aspect of her or his life. Why is such all-encompassing worship so hard to do?
- Do you think "contemporary worship" places special demands on musicians and poses special risks to them? If so, what?

# Why Study Anaheim Vineyard's Worship? A Guide for Different Disciplines and Areas of Interest

## *Christianity*

If you are interested in Christianity as a religion generally, then the Anaheim Vineyard is helpful for understanding . . .

- How popular religious movements arise in an American context;
- How primitivism (the desire to replicate the biblical church) and pragmatism (aiming for what works to replicate religious experience) often characterize these American movements, especially in Pentecostalism and its spinoffs;[1]
- The level of devotion to Jesus Christ typical among evangelical Christians;
- How worship itself can become one of the battlegrounds for "culture wars" if detractors of new musical forms demonize the pop quality of new worship music.

Here are discussion questions based on these general religious issues:

- Historian Nathan Hatch has suggested that the democratic culture of America allows for grass-roots religious movements to arise which have little connection to tradition and formal marks of church authority.[2] Was the Anaheim movement another example of the success of such a "popular" movement led by a strong, grass-roots minister?
- When do you think the Anaheim Vineyard congregation was trying to appropriate the power and life of the 1st century church, and when do you think it was drawing upon distinctly American ways of being Christian?
- Why do evangelicals often express their religious devotion to *God* specifically as attachment to *Jesus Christ*?
- If one saw pop or rock music as inherently rebellious, how might one have been threatened by the development of worship based on these forms of music?

1. Primitivism and pragmatism are categories used by Grant Wacker in *Heaven Below: Early Pentecostals and American Culture* (Cambridge: Harvard University Press, 2001).
2. Nathan Hatch, *The Democratization of American Christianity* (New Haven: Yale University Press, 1989).

## Christian Worship

If you are interested in worship generally, then the Anaheim Vineyard is helpful for understanding . . .

- The re-ordering of Protestant worship so that a long musical set becomes an extended time at the beginning of the service;
- One of the theological rationales given for the use of music in this way;
- Why musicians—and not pastors—came to be known as "worship leaders" in popular usage;
- The role of songs with simple lyrics, expressing great feeling, often addressed directly to God (or Christ), and done with repetition, in cultivating a strong sense of being in God's presence in worship;
- One of the sources of contemporary worship;
- How, in some churches, meaning in worship is not created by set structures of fixed order, written texts, and sacramental symbols but more by other means of evoking religious experience;
- How the influence of the Charismatic Movement or the Quaker spiritual tradition could reintroduce an emphasis upon the Holy Spirit's immediate activity in worship.

Here are discussion questions based on these general worship issues:

- Why was the term "worship" sometimes used as a synonym for singing or music in the Anaheim Vineyard congregation?
- Why is there a need to provide theological or biblical reasons for how music was used in the Anaheim Vineyard congregation? What are the strengths of Wimber's theological explanation of the multiple phases of worship?
- Why did Vineyard worshipers often closely link the sense of God's presence and power to the intimate love songs directed to him? Was God responding to their expressions of love, or was there something in the quality of the songs themselves that opened up a deepened sense of awareness?
- What did you see in the Anaheim Vineyard congregation's worship that seems replicated in "contemporary worship" in later decades? Do later appropriations retain the power and freshness of the Anaheim Vineyard, in your opinion, or do they lapse into their own forms of "tradition"?
- Beyond the issue of musical style, how might observers formed in more "liturgical" ways of worship miss the point of Vineyard worship and vice versa?[3]

3. See Melanie Ross, "Joseph's Britches Revisited: Reflections on Method in Liturgical Theology," *Worship* 80, no. 6 (November 2006): 528-50.

- How was the emphasis upon the Holy Spirit in this congregation's worship connected to the expectancy with which worshipers arrived for services?

## Evangelism and Discipleship

If you are interested in evangelism and discipleship, then the Anaheim Vineyard is helpful for understanding . . .

- The rise of a new "formula" for developing churches attractive to baby boomers: the use of pop music instruments, extended congregational singing using new expressive songs, and strong biblical and doctrinal teaching for the sermon;
- The early stages of a megachurch;
- The role of "signs and wonders," i.e., powerful demonstrations of divine power in gifts like healing and in supplementing spoken presentations of the Gospel within the Vineyard's ministry.

Here are discussion questions based on these evangelism and discipleship issues:

- What qualities of the Anaheim Vineyard and similar churches make this kind of Christianity appealing and accessible to so many?
- What evangelistic role do you think the social networking occurring in small groups and other behind-the-scenes venues play in complementing the public ministry occurring in worship services?
- Do you think the combination of "love songs to Jesus" and dramatic demonstrations of "signs and wonders" create a balance (or tension) between divine immanence and transcendence?

## Spirituality

If you are interested in spirituality, then the Anaheim Vineyard is helpful for understanding . . .
- The emphasis upon "intimacy" as a critical category for corporate worship, not just individual communing with God;
- A reliance upon congregational song to mediate a sense of God's presence in worship;
- The growing ability to replicate corporate worship experiences privately through easily available recordings of music;

- The level of devotion to Jesus Christ typical among evangelical Christians historically.

Here are discussion questions based on these spirituality issues:

- What are the points of continuity and discontinuity between the Vineyard's use of images for intimate fellowship with God and prior expressions of sensuality or romance in the history of Christian spirituality?
- Has the close connection between worship music and God's presence made music a new kind of "sacrament"?[4]
- Why do evangelicals often express their religious devotion to *God* specifically as attachment to *Jesus Christ*? Does the critical role that a personal experience of salvation has translate into devotional attachment to the Savior?

## *Preaching*

If you are interested in preaching, then the Anaheim Vineyard is helpful for understanding . . .

- how "preacher" and "teacher" can be closely related roles in a certain style of expository preaching;
- sermons which integrate relevance to the people, theology, and attentiveness to the Bible;
- communication dynamics.

Here are discussion questions based on these preaching issues:

- What is the difference between preaching and teaching? How does one know when one has heard a sermon or a lecture?
- With which of the following do you think Wimber showed the greatest ease: the Bible, theology, or understanding his listeners?
- How critical is it that the preacher create a sense of rapport with the congregation? Are there dangers both in failing to develop this connection and in overdeveloping it?

4. For a suggestion that it has done so, see chapter 8 in Swee Hong Lim and Lester Ruth, *Lovin' on Jesus: A Concise History of Contemporary Worship* (Nashville: Abingdon Press, forthcoming, 2017).

## Church History

If you are interested in church history, then the Anaheim Vineyard is helpful for understanding . . .

- A popular expression of a new church influenced by charismatic renewal;
- How a new charismatic-influenced church positioned itself to be distinguished from classic Pentecostalism;
- How evangelical popular religiosity found expression in indigenous musical forms crossing formal church structures;
- Another example of the role of Southern California in birthing new evangelical movements, a role that began in the early 20th century with the rise of Pentecostalism;

Here are discussion questions based on these church history issues:

- Is it inevitable that dynamic Christian renewal movements seek ways to stabilize and maintain their special, original qualities as time passes? Is this development good or bad?
- What distinguished the Anaheim Vineyard teaching from older Pentecostal positions about baptism in the Holy Spirit and speaking in tongues?
- Does the rise of music-based "contemporary worship" constitute its own special form of cross-denominational ecumenism? In what sense has the appropriation of new forms of worship made older denominational labels irrelevant on Sunday mornings?
- Could a case be made that, since the Azusa Street revival and the rise of Pentecostalism in Los Angeles in the early 20th century, Southern California has been one of the recurring centers for the development of new forms of Christianity? Why or why not?

## Sociology of Religion

If you are interested in sociology of religion, then the Anaheim Vineyard is helpful for understanding . . .

- How the phenomenon of identifying with a certain kind of music as a form of social identification in the mid-20th century got carried over into the church with the rise of new forms of worship;
- The participation of baby boomers in new kinds of American worship and churches in the second half of the 20th century;

- How some new churches of the period combined being theologically conservative and culturally progressive in worship;
- An example of a recurring phenomenon in American religiosity whereby democratic leveling allows greater ministry by lay people and easier access to experiencing the divine in profound ways;
- The flattening of denominational hierarchies in favor of pastor-led church networks.

Here are discussion questions based on these sociology of religion issues:

- How might the "worship wars" fought over worship style at the end of the 20th century have been in some respects a continuation of earlier generational conflicts?
- Is it significant that baby boomers would have ranged in age from late teens to early 30s when the Anaheim Vineyard publicly launched in 1977? In what ways should the origins of "new paradigm churches"[5] be attributed to the coming of age of this generation?
- Why is it that the Anaheim Vineyard congregation (theologically conservative yet progressive with the use of pop cultural forms) is the antithesis of some mainline liturgical churches (theologically liberal yet conservative in the use of pop cultural forms for worship)?
- Despite its popular pastor, how was it that the Anaheim Vineyard was in many respects a "people's" church?
- Will the pastor-led church networks springing from a "mother church" become the new denominations?

---

5. Donald E. Miller, *Reinventing American Protestantism: Christianity in the New Millennium* (Berkeley and Los Angeles: University of California Press, 1997).

# Glossary

**Calvary Chapel** A church in Costa Mesa, California, pastored by Chuck Smith, which spearheaded ministry to youth counterculture in the 1960s and 1970s. It became the "mother church" of a network of churches by the same name.

**Charismatic** Pentecostal-type Christianity that developed in the second half of the 20th century that differed from classic Pentecostalism in denominational affiliation, doctrine, or expression. Charismatic Christians appropriated from Pentecostal influence an emphasis upon an infilling or empowerment by the Holy Spirit along with an expectation that the Spirit's gifts (*charismata* in the original Greek) would be manifested in corporate and individual worship. Often, but not always, an emphasis was placed on speaking in tongues.

**Charismatic Movement or Charismatic Renewal Movement** As used in this volume, a spread of charismatic practices and piety in the 1960s and following among both new Christian movements and churches, e.g., the Jesus Movement and revitalization efforts among members of non-Pentecostal churches. In the latter case, charismatic members of these non-Pentecostal denominations often organized themselves to facilitate the spread of this spirituality, e.g., the United Methodist Renewal Services Fellowship.

**Church Growth Movement** An approach to evangelism and mission in the second half of the 20th century based on research into the social processes and factors which determine numerical success or failure in the mission field. Church Growth principles define the sociological aspects that usually accompany evangelistic success. Church Growth consultants are experts in these principles who can help churches understand and apply the principles.

**Five phases of worship** John Wimber's explanation of the appropriate progression in a worship service, especially in the opening musical segment. The goal of the phases is intimate communion with God and a life lived as an act of honoring God.

**Friends** The more formal name for Quakers, whose origins date from England in the 17th century.

**Fuller Theological Seminary** A large, multidenominational evangelical seminary whose main campus is located in Pasadena, California. Its School of World Mission was founded in the 1960s with a strong emphasis upon Church Growth principles.

**Interpretation** One of the supernatural gifts of the Holy Spirit by which a message delivered in tongues is interpreted by another worshiper for the understanding of the congregation.

**Intimacy (with God)** The desired end for a worshiper's experience in the Vineyard approach to worship. Intimacy involves a close sense of fellowship with God as well as a mutual exchange of intensely felt love between the worshiper and God.

**Jesus People** The name given to the members of the youth and hippie counterculture of the 1960s and 1970s who adopted Christianity.

**Jesus Movement** The various strands of Christianity that arose out of the conversion and organization of the Jesus People.

**Kinship group** The term the congregation used for its home fellowship and worship groups.

**Megachurch** A church with several thousand in attendance in weekly worship. The rise of these churches has proliferated in the second half of the 20th century.

**Ministry time** Commonly, the third—and last—segment in a Vineyard order of worship during which the Spirit of God is active among the congregation through the prayers and ministrations of worshipers to each other.

**Pentecostal** A type of Christianity, from the early 20th century, so named because its adherents see themselves as having recovered the power and phenomena of the original Pentecost. Key emphases include a distinct infilling of the Holy Spirit, an experience normally called "baptism in the Holy Spirit" after the terminology of the biblical book of Acts, and the evidence of the Holy Spirit by speaking in tongues. Pentecostals also affirm the manifestation of other spiritual gifts as listed in Scripture.

**Power evangelism** John Wimber's term for conversions precipitated by healings and miracles.

**Prophecy** One of the supernatural spiritual gifts demonstrated in corporate worship by which the Holy Spirit gives a message to an individual to deliver to others. A "prophetic word" is another name for the message which the Spirit has given.

**Quaker** See Friends.

**Signs and wonders** A shorthand way by which Wimber and others referred to supernatural manifestations given by the Holy Spirit.

**Singing in the Spirit** Singing in tongues.

**Speaking in tongues** As used in this volume, speech given supernaturally by the Holy Spirit which sounds unintelligible to the human ear. Speaking in tongues is also known as glossolalia after the Greek word in the New Testament for tongues or languages. Acts and 1 Corinthians are important scriptures for those who emphasize the experience. Some instances in Acts were in languages understood by bystanders.

**Spiritual gifts** Supernatural manifestations of the power of the Holy Spirit and the love of

God, often evidenced in worship. As listed in the New Testament, these would include prophecy, tongues, interpretation of tongues, and healing, among other gifts. Sometimes simply called "gifts" in this volume.

**Tongues** See speaking in tongues.

**Word of knowledge** Supernatural insight given to one person by the Holy Spirit of another's condition or circumstances.

**Worship** Musical expressions of praise and adoration to God in common Vineyard usage. Sometimes the term becomes synonymous with the opening period of congregational singing.

# Suggestions for Further Study

*Books, articles, dissertations, and published recordings:*

*Back to Our Roots: Stories of the Vineyard* (as told by Carol Wimber). DVD. Doin' the Stuff, 2006.

Dawson, Connie. "John Wimber: A Biographical Sketch of His Life and Ministry in America." Ph.D. diss., Regent University, 2012.

Fromm, Charles E. "Textual Communities and New Song in the Multimedia Age: The Routinization of Charisma in the Jesus Movement." Ph.D. diss., Fuller Theological Seminary, 2006.

*Horizons: Vineyard's Past, Present & Future.* DVD. Stafford, TX: Vineyard Resources.

Horton, Kenneth F. "The Vineyard Movement and Eschatology: An Interpretation." Ph.D. diss., Dallas Theological Seminary, 1999.

Hunt, Stephen. "The Anglican Wimberites." *Pneuma* 17, no.1 (1995): 105–18.

———. "'Doing the Stuff': The Vineyard Connection." In *Charismatic Christianity: Sociological Perspectives*, edited by Stephen Hunt, Malcolm Hamilton, and Tony Walter, 77-96. New York: St. Martin's Press, 1997.

Ingalls, Monique Marie. "Awesome in This Place: Sound, Space, and Identity in Contemporary North American Evangelical Worship." Ph.D. diss., University of Pennsylvania, 2008.

Jackson, Bill. *The Quest for the Radical Middle: A History of the Vineyard.* Cape Town: Vineyard International Publishing, 1999.

———. "A Short History of the Association of Vineyard Churches." In *Church, Identity, and Change: Theology and Denominational Structures in Unsettled Times*, edited by David A. Roozen and James R. Nieman. Grand Rapids: Eerdmans, 2005.

Koenig, Sarah. "This Is My Daily Bread: Toward a Sacramental Theology of Evangelical Praise and Worship." *Worship* 82, no. 2 (March 2008): 141–61.

Labanow, Cory E. *Evangelicalism and the Emerging Church: A Congregational Study of a Vineyard Church.* Farnham and Burlington: Ashgate, 2009.

Luhrmann, T. M. *When God Talks Back: Understanding the American Evangelical Relationship with God.* New York: Alfred A. Knopf, 2012.

Miller, Donald E. *Reinventing American Protestantism: Christianity in the New Millennium.* Berkeley and Los Angeles: University of California Press, 1997.

Nathan, Rich, and Ken Wilson. *Empowered Evangelicals: Bringing Together the Best of the Evangelical and Charismatic Worlds*. Ann Arbor: Vine Books, 1995.

Nekola, Anna E. "Between This World and the Next: The Musical 'Worship Wars' and Evangelical Ideology in the United States, 1960–2005." Ph.D. diss., University of Wisconsin-Madison, 2009.

———. "U.S. Evangelicals and the Redefinition of Worship Music." In *Mediating Faiths: Religion and Socio-Cultural Change in the Twenty-First Century*, edited by Michael Bailey and Guy Redden. Burlington: Ashgate Publishing Co., 2011.

Park, Andy. "The Birth of a Worship Movement." In *To Know You More: Cultivating the Heart of the Worship Leader*. Downers Grove, IL: InterVarsity Press, 2002.

Perrin, Robin Dale. "Signs and Wonders: The Growth of the Vineyard Christian Fellowship." PhD diss., Washington State University, 1989.

Redman, Robb. *The Great Worship Awakening: Singing a New Song in the Postmodern Church*. San Francisco: Jossey-Bass, 2002.

*Vineyard Roots Explained*. DVD. Yorba Linda: Vineyard Resource Center, 2012.

Williams, Don. "Theological Perspective and Reflection on the Vineyard Christian Fellowship." In *Church, Identity, and Change: Theology and Denominational Structures in Unsettled Times*, edited by David A. Roozen and James R. Nieman. Grand Rapids: Eerdmans, 2005.

Wimber, Carol. *John Wimber: The Way It Was*. London: Hodder and Stoughton, 1999.

Wimber, John. *Healing Seminar DVD*. 8-DVD set. Stafford, TX: Vineyard Resources, 2008.

———. *Signs, Wonders, and Church Growth*. 13-DVD set. Stafford, TX: Vineyard Resources, 2008.

———. *Worship*. 5-DVD set. Stafford, TX: Vineyard Resources.

———. "Zip to 3,000 in 5 Years." *Christian Life* 44, no. 6 (October 1982): 19–23.

*Winds of Worship Conference at Anaheim 1* and *2*. VHS tapes. Anaheim, CA: Vineyard Music Group, 1996.

Work, Telford. "Pentecostal and Charismatic Worship." In *The Oxford History of Christian Worship*, edited by Geoffrey Wainwright and Karen B. Westerfield Tucker, 574-85. New York: Oxford University Press, 2006.

Zichterman, Joseph T. "The Distinctives of John Wimber's Theology and Practice within the American Pentecostal-Charismatic Movement." Ph.D. diss., Trinity Evangelical Divinity School, 2011.

In addition to these written and videotaped sources, the reader seeking further information is directed to the following resources:

The first Vineyard album, recorded in 1982, was *All the Earth Shall Worship: Worship Songs of the Vineyard*, released by Mercy Records.

Many clips of John Wimber speaking are available on YouTube.com.

A variety of recordings and publications related to John Wimber and the Vineyard can be found for purchase at http://www.vineyardresources.com/equip/.

Many of the papers of John Wimber are found in the John Wimber Collection in the library archives at Regent University in Virginia Beach, Virginia.

Debate has sometimes waged both within and beyond John Wimber's ministry about "signs and wonders." Readers wanting cordial treatments of the various issues involved along with different Christian perspectives are encouraged to consider the works below:

Grudem, Wayne A. *Are Miraculous Gifts for Today? Four Views*. Grand Rapids: Zondervan, 1996.

Smedes, Lewis B., ed. *Ministry and the Miraculous: A Case Study at Fuller Theological Seminary*. Pasadena: Fuller Theological Seminary, 1987.

A thoughtful, vigorous Vineyard apologetic can be found in the following:

Nathan, Rich, and Ken Wilson. *Empowered Evangelicals: Bringing Together the Best of the Evangelical and Charismatic Worlds*. Boise, ID: Ampelon Publishing, 1995 and 2009.

# Works Cited

*Authentic Worship in a Changing Culture.* Grand Rapids: CRC Publications, 1997.

Barclay, Robert. *An Apology for the True Christian Divinity.* 1678.

Bergler, Thomas E. "'I Found My Thrill': The Youth for Christ Movement and American Congregational Singing, 1940–1970." In *Wonderful Words of Life: Hymns in American Protestant History & Theology,* edited by Richard J. Mouw and Mark A. Noll, 123-49. Grand Rapids: Eerdmans, 2004.

————. *The Juvenilization of American Christianity.* Grand Rapids: Eerdmans, 2012.

Black, Kathy. *Worship Across Cultures: A Handbook.* Nashville: Abingdon Press, 1998.

Bloy, Myron B., Jr., ed. *Multi-Media Worship: A Model and Nine Viewpoints.* New York: The Seabury Press, 1969.

Briggs, Kenneth A. "More Churches Quietly Forging Independent Paths." *New York Times,* May 10, 1981, 26.

Bugnini, Annibale. *The Reform of the Liturgy, 1948–1975.* Translated by Matthew J. O'Connell. Collegeville, MN: Liturgical Press, 1990.

Butler, Jon, Grant Wacker, and Randall Balmer. *Religion in American Life: A Short History.* 2nd ed. Oxford and New York: Oxford University Press, 2011.

Di Sabatino, David. *Frisbee: The Life and Death of a Hippie Preacher.* DVD. Garden Grove, CA: Jester Media, 2006.

————. *The Jesus People Movement: An Annotated Bibliography and General Resource.* Lake Forest, IL: Jester Media, 2004.

————. "The Unforgettable Fire: Pentecostals and the Role of Experience in Worship." *Worship Leader* 9, no. 6 (November/December 2000): 20–23.

Enroth, Ronald M., Edward E. Ericson, Jr., and C. Breckinridge Peters. *The Jesus People.* Grand Rapids: Eerdmans, 1972.

Fromm, Charles E. "Textual Communities and New Song in the Multimedia Age: The Routinization of Charisma in the Jesus Movement." Ph.D. diss., Fuller Theological Seminary, 2006.

Hamilton, Michael. "The Triumph of the Praise Songs: How Guitars Beat Out the Organ in the Worship Wars." *Christianity Today* 43, no. 8 (July 12, 1999): 29–35.

Hatch, Nathan. *The Democratization of American Christianity.* New Haven: Yale University Press, 1989.

Hunter, George G. *Church for the Unchurched*. Nashville: Abingdon Press, 1996.

Ingalls, Monique. "Transnational Connections, Musical Meaning, and the 1990s 'British Invasion' of North American Evangelical Worship Music." In *The Oxford Handbook of Music and World Christianities*, edited by Suzel Ana Reily and Jonathan Dueck, 425-48. Oxford and New York: Oxford University Press, 2016.

Jackson, Bill. *The Quest for the Radical Middle: A History of the Vineyard*. Cape Town: Vineyard International Publishing, 1999.

———. "A Short History of the Association of Vineyard Churches." In *Church, Identity, and Change: Theology and Denominational Structures in Unsettled Times*, edited by David A. Roozen and James R. Nieman. Grand Rapids: Eerdmans, 2005.

Johnson, Todd. "Disconnected Rituals: The Origins of the Seeker Service Movement." In *The Conviction of Things Not Seen: Worship and Ministry in the 21st Century*, edited by Todd E. Johnson. Grand Rapids: Brazos, 2002.

John Wimber Collection. Accessed September 8, 2008, and August 24, 2016. http://www.regent.edu/lib/special-collections/wimber-collection.cfm.

Koenig, Sarah. "This Is My Daily Bread: Toward a Sacramental Theology of Evangelical Praise and Worship." *Worship* 82, no. 2 (March 2008): 141–61.

Lim, Swee Hong, and Lester Ruth. *Lovin' on Jesus: A Concise History of Contemporary Worship*. Nashville: Abingdon Press, forthcoming, 2017.

Long, Thomas G. *Beyond the Worship Wars: Building Vital and Faithful Worship*. Bethesda, MD: The Alban Institute, 2001.

Miller, Donald E. *Reinventing American Protestantism: Christianity in the New Millennium*. Berkeley and Los Angeles: University of California Press, 1997.

Park, Andy. *The Worship Journey: A Quest of Heart, Mind, and Strength*. Woodinville, WA: Augustus Ink Books, 2010.

———. *To Know You More: Cultivating the Heart of the Worship Leader*. Downers Grove, IL: InterVarsity Press, 2002.

Patterson, Ben. "Cause for Concern." In Tim Stafford, "Testing the Wine from John Wimber's Vineyard." *Christianity Today* 30, no. 11 (August 8, 1986): 20.

Pecklers, Keith F. *Liturgy: The Illustrated History*. Mahwah, NJ: Paulist Press, 2012.

Plantinga, Cornelius, Jr., and Sue A. Rozeboom. *Discerning the Spirits: A Guide to Thinking about Christian Worship Today*. Grand Rapids: Eerdmans, 2003.

Redman, Robb. *The Great Worship Awakening: Singing a New Song in the Postmodern Church*. San Francisco: Jossey-Bass, 2002.

Ross, Melanie. "Joseph's Britches Revisited: Reflections on Method in Liturgical Theology." *Worship* 80, no. 6 (November 2006): 528–50.

Ruth, Lester. "Lex Agendi, Lex Orandi: Toward an Understanding of Seeker Services as a New Kind of Liturgy." *Worship* 70, no. 5 (September 1996): 386–405.

Senn, Frank C. *Christian Liturgy: Catholic and Evangelical.* Minneapolis: Fortress Press, 1997.

Smedes, Lewis B., ed. *Ministry and the Miraculous: A Case Study at Fuller Theological Seminary.* Pasadena, CA: Fuller Theological Seminary, 1987.

Smith, Chuck, and Tal Brooke. *Harvest.* Costa Mesa, CA: The Word for Today, 1987.

Spinks, Bryan D. *The Worship Mall: Contemporary Responses to Contemporary Culture.* New York: Church Publishing, Inc., 2011.

Stafford, Tim. "Testing the Wine from John Wimber's Vineyard." *Christianity Today* 30, no. 11 (August 8, 1986), 17-22.

Steven, James. "The Spirit in Contemporary Charismatic Worship." In *The Spirit in Worship— Worship in the Spirit*, edited by Teresa Berger and Bryan D. Spinks, 245-59. Collegeville, MN: Liturgical Press, 2009.

Townend, Stuart. "The Musician in Revival." *Worship Together: A Resource Magazine for Worship Leaders, Pastors, and Musicians* 10 (1994): 4-6.

*Vineyard Roots Explained.* DVD. Yorba Linda: Vineyard Resource Center, 2012.

Wacker, Grant. *Heaven Below: Early Pentecostals and American Culture.* Cambridge: Harvard University Press, 2001.

Wagner, C. P. "Vineyard Christian Fellowship." In *The New International Dictionary of Pentecostal and Charismatic Movements,* edited by Stanley M. Burgess et al. Grand Rapids: Zondervan, 2002.

Ward, Pete. *Selling Worship: How What We Sing Has Changed the Church.* Bletchley: Paternoster Press, 2005.

*What God Hath Wrought: Chuck Smith, "The Father of the Jesus Movement."* DVD produced by Jurgen and Stacey Peretzki. West Hills, CA: Screen Savers Entertainment, 2012.

White, James F. *Protestant Worship: Traditions in Transition.* Louisville: Westminster/John Knox Press, 1989.

————. *Roman Catholic Worship: Trent to Today.* New York: Paulist Press, 1995.

Williams, Don. "Historical-Theological Perspective and Reflection on John Wimber and the Vineyard." Accessed July 4, 2008, January 16, 2013, and August 30, 2016. http://vineyard indonesia.org/index.php?option=com_content&view=article&id=45%3Aborneo&catid=1%3 Alatest&showall=1.

————. "Theological Perspective and Reflection on the Vineyard Christian Fellowship." In *Church, Identity, and Change: Theology and Denominational Structures in Unsettled Times*, edited by David A. Roozen and James R. Nieman. Grand Rapids: Eerdmans, 2005.

Wimber, Carol. "The Flame of God's Presence." In *The Way In Is the Way On*. Atlanta: Ampelon Publishing, 2006.

Wimber, John. "Don't Lose Your First Love." In *The Ministry and Teachings of John Wimber* series, CD #310. Doin' the Stuff/Vineyard Music Group, 2004.

————. "Essence of Worship." In *The Ministry and Teachings of John Wimber* series, CD #311. Doin' the Stuff/Vineyard Music Group, 2004.

————. "The Life-Changing Power of Worship." In *All About Worship: Insights and Perspectives on Worship*, edited by Julie Bogart. Anaheim, CA: Vineyard Music Group, 1998.

————. "Loving God." In *The Ministry and Teachings of John Wimber* series, CD #303. Doin' the Stuff/Vineyard Music Group, 2004.

————. *The Way In Is the Way On: John Wimber's Teachings and Writings on Life in Christ.* Atlanta: Ampelon Publishing, 2006.

————. "Why Do We Worship?" In *The Ministry and Teachings of John Wimber* series, CD #9892. Doin' the Stuff/Vineyard Music Group, 2004.

————. "Worship: Intimacy with God." In *Thoughts on Worship*, edited by John Wimber. Anaheim, CA: Vineyard Music Group, 1996.

————. "Zip to 3,000 in 5 Years." *Christian Life* 44, no. 6 (October 1982): 19–23.

Witvliet, John D. "The Blessing and Bane of the North American Mega-Church: Implications for Twenty-First Century Congregational Song." *Jahrbuch fur Liturgik und Hymnologie* (1998): 196–213.

Work, Telford. "Pentecostal and Charismatic Worship." In *The Oxford History of Christian Worship*, edited by Geoffrey Wainwright and Karen B. Westerfield Tucker, 574-85. New York: Oxford University Press, 2006.

# Index

Calvary Chapel, 3, 5, 9, 10, 11, 13, 14, 15, 16, 19, 20, 25, 31, 33, 34, 40, 45, 67, 72, 85, 104, 105, 116, 117, 128

Canyon High School, 9, 14, 31, 38, 47, 48, 58, 59, 69, 74, 76, 86

Charismatic, 4, 5, 8, 9, 10, 12, 17, 20, 22, 33, 40, 41, 56, 70, 73, 74, 75, 78, 80, 87, 98, 106, 115, 133, 136

Church Growth, 8, 10, 13, 14, 17, 31, 39, 45, 66, 93, 116

Contemporary worship, 3, 4, 5, 8, 9, 11, 15, 45, 81, 83, 85, 128, 130, 131, 133, 135, 136

Friends (Quaker), 9, 10, 13, 14, 32, 33, 46

Frisbee, Lonnie, 14, 40, 56

Fuller Theological Seminary, 5, 8, 10, 13, 14, 16, 17, 32, 39, 45, 72, 93, 121, 122

Gulliksen, Kenn, 10, 13, 14, 21, 31

Healing, 5, 9, 14, 17, 22, 23, 37, 38, 39, 40, 42, 43, 44, 53, 55, 63, 74, 75, 78, 79, 80, 119, 121, 122, 134

Holy Spirit, 3, 5, 8, 9, 11, 12, 14, 17, 22, 24, 25, 29, 30, 31, 34, 35, 38, 39, 40, 41, 42, 43, 64, 65, 68, 69, 70, 71, 73, 74, 75, 77, 78, 79, 80, 89, 100, 106, 108, 110, 126, 130, 133, 134, 136

Intimacy (with God), 3, 4, 9, 10, 22, 29, 30, 34, 36, 38, 39, 41, 44, 45, 64, 66, 67, 68, 69, 74, 112, 113, 118, 120

Jesus People, 9, 16, 20, 25, 33, 35, 40, 56, 104

Kingdom of God, 9, 34, 42, 43, 44

Kinship group, 25, 39, 53, 57, 65, 66, 77, 80, 117

Maranatha! Music, 5, 9, 13, 72, 85, 128

Megachurch, 8, 17, 128, 134

Payne, Gunner, 10, 12, 32

Pentecostal, 5, 8, 10, 12, 17, 33, 40, 69, 72, 74, 75, 78, 99, 106, 115, 116, 118, 132, 136

Phases of worship, 99, 117, 118, 119, 120, 133

Power evangelism, 23, 40, 41

Prophecy, 9, 38, 43, 65, 76, 99

Signs and wonders, 24, 45, 110, 134

Smith, Chuck, 9, 16, 19, 40, 72, 104

Speaking in tongues, 8, 9, 17, 44, 98, 99, 100, 101, 110, 136

Spiritual gifts, 9, 11, 17, 22, 25, 30, 38, 39, 40, 76, 99

Tuttle, Carl, 3, 4, 9, 13, 15, 21, 32, 37, 42, 49, 55, 64, 66, 69, 70, 71, 86, 109, 110, 112, 117, 119

Wagner, Peter, 5, 13, 32, 40, 76, 77

Wimber, Carol, 10, 12, 13, 21, 32, 33, 64, 66, 70, 71, 73, 79, 87

Word of knowledge, 45, 76